SCHOLASTIC

D1810477

Data Handling
Across the Curriculum

Everything you need to handle data in any subject

Year 5

Ann Montague-Smith

Full graphing toolkit and whiteboard resources included

Book End, Range Road, Witney, Oxfordshire, OX29 OYD

www.scholastic.co.uk

© 2012, Scholastic Ltd

1 2 3 4 5 6 7 8 9   0 1 2 3 4 5 6 7 8 9

British Library Cataloguing-in-Publication Data
A catalogue record for this book is available from the
British Library.

ISBN 978-1407-12523-7
Printed by Bell & Bain
CD duplicated by Media Plant
Text © 2012 Ann Montague-Smith and Julia Stanton

Due to the nature of the web we cannot guarantee the
content or links of any site mentioned. We strongly
recommend that teachers check websites before using
them in the classroom.

Authors
Ann Montague-Smith and Julia Stanton

Commissioning Editor
Paul Naish

Development Editors
Kate Pedlar and Pollyanna Poulter

Editors
Niamh O'Carroll and Rhiannon Findlay

Series Designer
Sarah Garbett and Andrea Lewis

Designer
Ricky Capanni (International Book Management)

Illustrator
International Book Management

Credits & Acknowledgements
© Crown copyright material is reproduced under the terms of the
Click Use Licence.

Cover image © Sashkin/Shutterstock.com

Contents

Introduction to Scholastic Data Handling

About the series

Scholastic Data Handling is designed to support primary teachers by helping their students in using important data-handling skills every day. Each title in the series provides opportunities for using relevant data within all subject areas, as defined by the National Curriculum. By using the series, a teacher or school can be confident that they are embedding data handling, so that children are given real opportunities to find data from sources such as other people, books and the internet, and to use data in a variety of practical ways.

The importance of data handling

Every day we encounter data. This might be through television programmes, internet searches to find the best price for something, comparing costs in shops, and in discussions with others. Children will come across data from very early on, such as how many grapes each of them in a group has, how tall their tower of bricks is compared with those of others, and so on. As children become older and develop their own interests, they will encounter data in areas such as sports and their results, shopping and getting good value for money, or where they might go on holiday.

In order to foster development in data handling, children need to experience using real data, in real-life situations, as often as possible, so that they make the connections between what they learn at school and life outside school. Eventually, when children leave education and begin employment, data-handling skills will be vital to them in managing their work and living in society.

About this book

This book provides full coverage of the Data Handling strand from the Primary National Strategy: *Framework for Teaching Mathematics.*

Each double-page lesson consists of one page with lesson details and a second, photocopiable, activity sheet typically showing a data-handling diagram, chart or graph. Where possible, data-handling software, such as a graphing or pictogram tool, is incorporated into the lesson. Children's own data can be captured using this software, then displayed on the interactive whiteboard for all to see and discuss.

Across the series, each area of the National Curriculum is visited. If a subject area does not lend itself well to realistic data for a certain age range, this has been left for a later book to ensure the data is always pertinent.

Lesson structure

Each lesson contains:

- Mathematics objective(s) for the relevant year group taken from the Primary National Strategy for Mathematics and the National Curriculum. At least one objective from the data-handling strand is included for every lesson. National Curriculum objectives have been abbreviated, but full details can be found on a planning grid in the 'planning' area of the CD-ROM. Subject-specific objective(s) taken from the National Curriculum requirements or guidelines for the subject.
- The vocabulary that specifically relates to the data handling content of the lesson.
- A list of resources, including practical materials, activity sheets that can be displayed or printed and references to images and interactive data-handling tools on the CD-ROM.

Resources
- Seeds, such as sunflower or runner bean; pots, compost, gardening equipment; uniform non-standard units of length, such as interlocking cubes

CD-ROM slideshow: ✎
- Activity sheets: 'Growing seeds – table' (two copies for each child), 'Growing seeds block graph' (two copies for each child) and 'Sunflower challenge' (also p37)
- Images: 'Growing sunflower'; 'Growing seeds'
- Block graph tool

- An introduction to the lesson, including questions to ask the children about the topic and the data.
- The children's task, which may be for group, paired or individual work.
- Differentiation to help you decide how to help the less confident learners in your group or class, and how to extend the learning for the more confident.
- A review of the lesson, where children's work may be considered, or where further data is introduced. This section includes more questions to ask the children in order to identify their level of understanding.
- A 'Now try this…' section, which has further ideas for activities based on the curriculum topic and its data-handling possibilities.
- CD-ROM follow-up material, which consists of images to stimulate enquiry or use of the data-handling tools to extend the investigation.
- An activity sheet with material which may form part of the Introduction, the Children's task or the Review.

How to use the CD-ROM

- The CD-ROM needs to be installed. Double-click the 'installDHYear5.exe' file, and follow the instructions onscreen to install the software to your network or computer. If you or your school has purchased more than one *Scholastic Data Handling* title, these will all feed into the same, single, *Scholastic Data Handling* program.
- The opening menu asks you to choose between a Teacher Zone and a Kids Zone.

Kids Zone

- The Kids Zone comprises eight maths tools to create and print sorting and Venn diagrams, Carroll diagrams, pictograms, tables and charts, block graphs, bar charts, line graphs and pie charts.

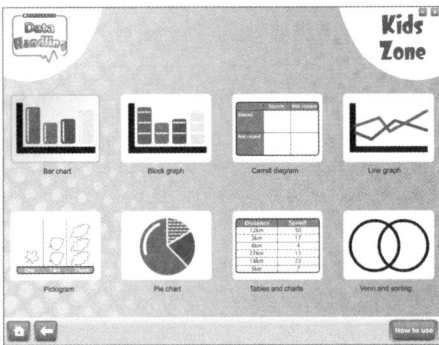

Teacher Zone

- **The Teacher Zone is password-protected. The password is: login.**
- Once in this zone, the relevant year group can be selected, which takes you to a lesson menu. There is at least one ready-made slideshow per lesson that includes all the CD-ROM resources needed: images, activity sheets, readymade 'interactive' graphs, Word documents and so on.

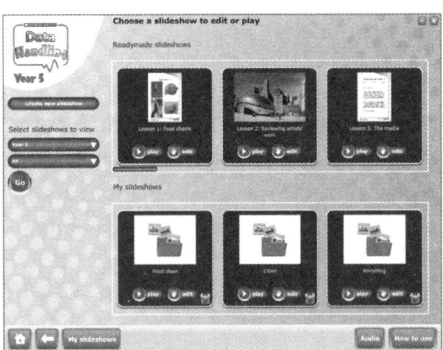

- It is possible to edit or create bespoke slideshows, selecting from all the resources provided for all years that have been installed. It is also possible to upload your own resources into the *Scholastic Data Handling* program. Bespoke slideshows are saved in the 'My slideshows' area.

Slideshow resources across the series include:
- Activity sheets as PDF files that can be printed or displayed, and editable activity sheets in Word or Excel. Images and video which can be displayed on a computer or interactive whiteboard.
- The same tools provided in the Kids Zone, as well as up to ten readymade 'interactives'.

A more detailed 'How to use' document is provided on the CD-ROM.

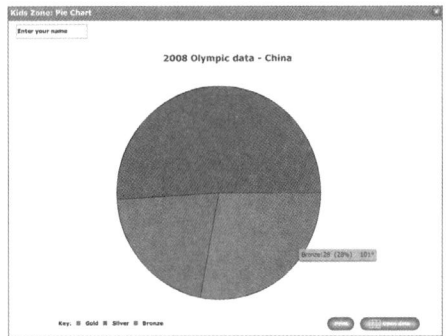

How to integrate data handling within a cross-curricular approach

When data handling is used as part of a topic or investigation, it gives children some insights into how they can use what they know in different curriculum areas, and in real life. The data handling in this series of books evolves naturally from the topics. In this way the children will experience data that is realistic, and relevant to them. Similarly, the 'Now try this...' section of the lessons gives further examples of collecting and using data in real-life situations. Within any topic there will be specific aspects of handling data that fit well within the subject matter. It is much better to use those aspects of handling data where they arise naturally, rather than try to 'force' data from topics.

This book provides opportunities for children to collect data, then organise it. There are opportunities to make tables, diagrams and graphs, as appropriate to the topic. There are also lots of opportunities to ask questions about the data, and to compare the class or individual children's data with that contained in the tables or graphs on the photocopiable pages provided in the book and on the CD-ROM.

Food chains

Mathematics learning objectives
Framework:
- **U&A:** Explain reasoning using diagrams, graphs and text; refine ways of recording using images and symbols.
- **HD:** Answer a set of related questions by collecting, selecting and organising relevant data; draw conclusions, using ICT to present features, and identify further questions to ask.
- **NC:** Ma4, 1a; Ma4, 2a–c

Science learning objectives (NC)
Sc2, 5d: To use food chains to show feeding relationships in a habitat.
Sc2, 5e: About how nearly all food chains start with a green plant.

. . . .

Vocabulary
Classify, diagram

Resources
- Books about animals and/or access to the internet

CD-ROM: 💿
- Activity sheets: 'Food chain' 1–3, 'Food chain cards', 'Our food chains', 'Our food chains answers', 'More food chains' (also p7) and 'Pets' food chain'
- Images: 'Food chain' 1–4, 'Producer' 1–6 and 'Predator' 1–4

Introduction
Display the activity sheet 'Food chain – 1' and explain that these are items which form a food chain. Ask:
- *To start our chain, who eats the lettuce?*
- *Who eats the slug/frog?*

Reveal the 'Food chain' images and the activity sheet 'Food chain – 2'. Explain that food chains begin with a plant. Discuss how a plant is a producer (it makes its own food) and that those who eat something are consumers. A predator eats other animals. Ask:
- *In this food chain, who is the producer?*
- *Who are predators/the prey?*

Explain that in some food chains one animal can be the top of the food chain because no other animal eats it. Ask the children to think of an example (lions, humans).

Display 'Food chain – 3'. Ask the children to work in pairs and put the food chain into sentences. Ask:

- *What is the producer?*
- *How would you describe the rabbit/fox?*

Explain that some animals eat both plants and meat. Introduce the word 'omnivore' and ask the children to suggest an animal (humans).

Children's task
Provide reference books about food chains. Ask the children to work in pairs with copies of the activity sheets 'Food chain cards' and 'Our food chains' (a version with answers is provided). They cut out the cards and make food chains from these; then copy their food chains onto 'Our food chains'. The children then decide on another animal, research that animal's food chains, and write (and illustrate) the animal's food chain.

Differentiation
More confident: Challenge the children to make food chains for several animals that they research.
Less confident: Ask the children to find the three food chains from 'Food chain cards'. Work as a group to find the food chain for another animal, such as a goat or a rat.

Review
Invite children to share their food chains. Ask:
- *Which animal is top of this food chain?*
- *Which is the producer/consumers?*
- *Who is the prey for the…?*

Then ask children to state which other animal they chose and what they found out about its food chain.

Display the activity sheet 'More food chains'. Repeat the questions above for each food chain. Look in particular at the final food chain and ask:
- *What is top of this food chain?*
- *So which animal is the prey?*
- *And which is the producer?*

Display the 'Producer' images from the CD-ROM. Explain that phytoplankton is a producer, using photosynthesis, as is algae. Zooplankton is a consumer. Discuss how food chains can begin with the animal and work down to the producer.

Now try this...
Ask the children to choose a pet and find out about its food chain in the wild, using the activity sheet 'Pets' food chain'. Make a display of the food chain diagrams and compare these with what we give pets to eat today.

CD-ROM follow-up material
Display the 'Predator' images from the CD-ROM and ask pairs of children to make a food chain using one of the animals as the beginning or the end of it. Challenge the children to find the longest food chain they can.

More food chains

■ Look carefully at these food chains.

grass → grasshopper → mouse → owl

phytoplankton → zooplankton → fish → seal → great white shark

algae → shrimp → fish → seal → polar bear

lion ← zebra ← grass

Reviewing artists' work

Mathematics learning objectives
Framework:
- **HD:** Answer a set of related questions by collecting, selecting and organising relevant data; draw conclusions, using ICT to present features, and identify further questions to ask.
- **NC:** Ma4, 1a; Ma4, 2b

Art and design learning objectives (NC)
- **3a:** Compare ideas, methods and approaches in their own and others' work and say what they think and feel about them.

. . . .

Vocabulary
Bar chart, chart

Resources
- Materials to make artworks in the chosen medium.
CD-ROM:
- Activity sheets: 'Reviewing artists' work', 'My work', 'Our class's work', 'Artworks by Class 5' (also p9), 'Reviewing artworks' and 'Timeline'
- Word® files: 'Our class's work' and 'Reviewing artworks'
- Images: 'Sculpture' 1–7

Introduction
This activity will take more than one lesson to complete, as it includes designing, making and evaluating a finished artwork. Display the first sculpture image, with the caption turned off, and provide copies of the activity sheet 'Reviewing artists' work'. Ask the children to study the image; then write their thoughts on the sheet. Discuss what they have written, asking questions such as:
- *Why do you think that?*
- *Who thought something different?*
Turn the caption on to reveal details about the sculpture. Repeat this with the other sculpture images.

Children's task
Decide which media the children want to use and provide the materials. Ask the children to use one of the artworks that they have discussed as their inspiration. They plan what to make, making sketches of their ideas; then create their images or artefacts.

Encourage them to review what they do at each stage, and to improve and adapt their work so that what they produce is of a good standard.

When all the work is finished, ask the children to create an exhibition. They add a card from the activity sheet 'My work' with their name and the title of their work, along with a description of their inspiration.

Ask the children to complete the activity sheet 'Our class's work' (also available as a Word® file), explaining what they think each work is about and what they like about it. Decide whether to ask them to evaluate everyone's work, or a group. Remind them to write briefly and succinctly in the available space.

Differentiation
More confident: Challenge the children to write evaluations that include constructive comments, written in such a manner as to cause no offence.
Less confident: Ask the children to review up to four works by other children and to write in a style that will cause no offence.

Review
Before the review, read the completed activity sheets 'Our class's work'. Choose those which give good, constructive comments and display these to the class. Ask the children to read through the first one. Ask:
- *In what ways are these helpful comments?*
- (Looking at the artwork) *What else could we say to the artist?*
Discuss with the children the range of artworks that they have done during the last year and make a list of these. Now display the activity sheet 'Artworks by Class 5'. Ask, for example:
- *What is the scale?*
- *How do you know this?*
- *How similar is this to the work that we do?*
- *What is different about what the children have done from what you have completed?*
- *How many works did the class complete in total?*
- *How did you work that out?*

Now try this...
Arrange a visit to a local art gallery or museum to study the sculptures. Ask the children to review each of the pieces that you name for them, using the activity sheet or Word® file 'Reviewing artworks'.

 CD-ROM follow-up material
Using the activity sheet 'Timeline', ask children to research each of the sculptors and place them on the timeline, explaining that if they are still alive their bars continue to the end of the grid. Children can use websites such as www.sculpture.org.uk for research.

Scholastic Data Handling Year 5

Artworks by Class 5

Scale: 1 : 5

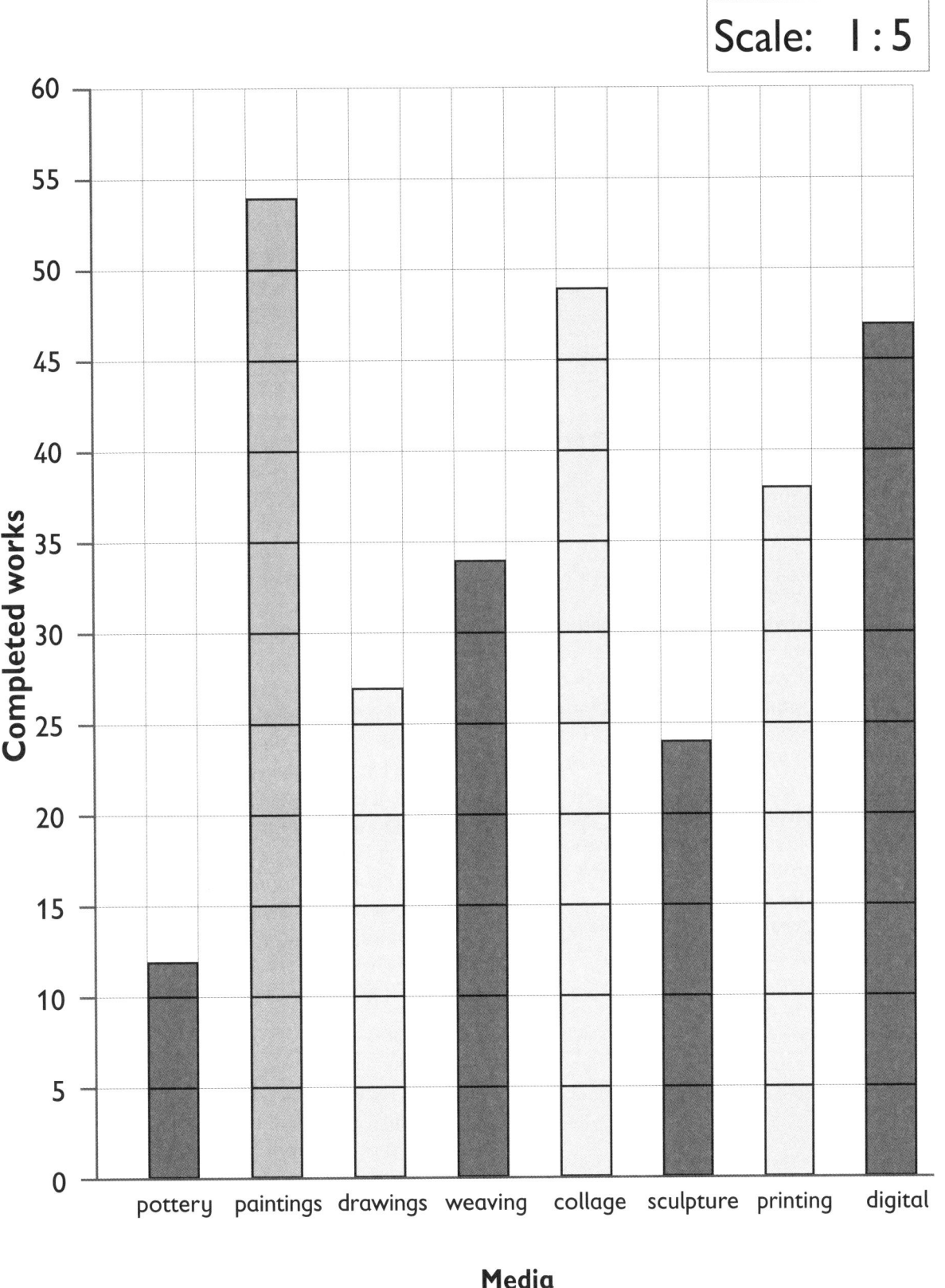

The media

Mathematics learning objectives
Framework:
- **HD:** Describe the occurrence of familiar events using the language of chance or likelihood.
- **NC:** Ma4, 1a; Ma4, 2a; Ma4, 2f

English learning objective (NC)
- **En2, 3f:** Distinguish between fact and opinion (for example, by looking at the purpose of the text, the reliability of information).

Vocabulary
Chart, impossible, possible, probable, probability

Resources
- Examples of various media, traditional and digital

CD-ROM:
- Activity sheets: 'Stories from the media' 1–3, 'Media stories' 1 and 2 , 'Are they true?' (also p11) and 'My news stories'
- Word® file: 'My news stories'
- Images: 'Headlines' 1–4

Introduction
Explain that in this activity the children will be considering some stories which have been published in the media. However, not all of these may be true, as some forms of media, for example the internet, publish stories which are jokes rather than real news stories.

Begin by displaying the activity sheet 'Stories from the media – 1'. Ask the children to note that there is a probability scale at the top of the screen. Ask them to read the story through; then discuss it with their partner. Ask the children to decide where they think the story fits on the probability scale. Discuss the story together, and ask questions such as:
- *Where do you think this story fits on the probability scale?*
- *Why do you think that?*
- *Who disagrees?*
- *What do you think about this story?*

Repeat this for the other two 'Stories from the media' activity sheets. As bizarre as it may seem, all of the stories appeared on Reuters' website in December 2010.

Children's task
Ask the children to work in pairs. They will each need a copy of activity sheets 'Media stories' 1 and 2. They read the first story; then discuss its content and decide what the probability is of the story being true. They repeat this for each of the other three stories. Ask the children to be ready to discuss their decisions during the review.

Differentiation
More confident: Challenge the children to find other unusual stories and to determine whether they believe these to be probable, possible or impossible, and why.
Less confident: Decide whether to work as a group to discuss each of the stories and to determine the probability for each one. Encourage the children to explain their reasoning.

Review
Review the stories from the activity sheets 'Media stories' 1 and 2. Please note that each of these stories was reported on news bulletins or the internet. Ask the children to explain what they thought of each of the stories, whether they thought each story was true, and what the likelihood was of the events really happening. The story of the burglar and the householder's response will probably need to be discussed in some detail, as there are moral and legal issues here in what was purported to have happened. Ask questions about each story such as:
- *Do you think this really happened?*
- *Why do you think that?*
- *So what is the probability of this having happened?*

Display the activity sheet 'Are they true?' Ask the children to read each story with a partner; then decide whether Class 5 classified the stories correctly. Ask questions such as:
- *Do you believe this story really happened?*
- *Why do you think that?*
- *How would you classify this story?*
- *What is the probability of it being true?*

If anyone asks, each of these stories was reported on the internet from a news source.

Now try this...
Ask the children to collect interesting and unusual news stories. These can be collected from local and national papers, magazines and the internet and recorded on the activity sheet or Word® version of 'My news stories'.

CD-ROM follow-up material
Display the images 'Headlines' 1–4 from the CD-ROM. Ask pairs of children to choose one headline and then each write a different story, one as a probable story and the other as an improbable story. Display them together with the headline. The blank masthead could also be used for children to write their own headline.

Are they true?

- Class 5 decided on the probability for these stories.
- Read the stories, then decide whether Class 5 has classified them correctly.

News story	Probable	Possible	Impossible
Biologically based LEDs are to be used instead of street lights. Glowing sea-urchin-shaped bio light emitting diodes have been planted inside the leaves of a plant. The new lights could replace electrically powered street lights, and the trees would help to remove carbon dioxide from the atmosphere.			✓
How about a special Christmas present? For £4.5 million you can have a full-size, non-flying Space Shuttle Orbiter replica made to the dimensions of the original ones. A full interior is available at an extra cost. You will be responsible for shipping and set-up costs.		✓	
A lady in the USA was riding on her ride-on lawnmower. She hit a pothole and was thrown about 5m ahead of the still-moving machine. As she lay unconscious the machine ran over her legs. Luckily she was found and taken to hospital where she recovered.	✓		

Make a model lighthouse

Mathematics learning objectives
Framework:
- **HD:** Answer a set of related questions by collecting, selecting and organising relevant data; draw conclusions, using ICT to present features, and identify further questions to ask.
- **NC:** Ma4, 1a; Ma4, 2a–c

Science learning objective (NC)
- **Sc4, 1a:** To construct circuits, incorporating a battery or power supply and a range of switches, to make electrical devices work (for example, buzzers, motors).

Vocabulary
Bar chart, chart, table

Resources
- Electrical wire, bulbs, batteries, switches and materials from which children can make their lighthouse or wheeled model, including kits and recyclable materials, and internet access

CD-ROM: 💿
- Activity sheets: 'Electric circuits', 'Our lighthouse', 'Our lighthouse review', 'Review of the models' (enlarged to A3), 'Sam's lighthouse' (also p13), 'Our model' and 'Height of lighthouses'
- Word® files: 'Our lighthouse review' and 'Review of the models'
- Images: 'Lighthouse' 1–5
- Video: 'Lighthouse'
- Bar chart tool

Introduction
Explain that the children will be designing and making a model lighthouse with a working light. Revise making electric circuits. Discuss how to wire up a circuit that includes both a light and a switch and ask children to draw a diagram of an electric circuit including a bulb and a switch. Ask questions such as:
- *What do you need in your circuit to make a bulb light?*

Display the activity sheet 'Electric circuits'. This shows three electric circuits, two will light the bulb. Ask questions such as:
- *Which circuit/s will/will not light the bulb? Why?*

Children's task
Display the lighthouse images and video from the CD-ROM. Ask the children to discuss them in pairs. Provide copies of the activity sheet 'Our lighthouse' for each pair to plan how to make their model lighthouse. They sketch how they want their lighthouse to look, draw the circuit diagram for lighting the bulb, and list the materials they will need. Ask the children to review their plan, check their written instructions and list of materials. Ask them to continue to review their plan as they make their model. Remind them that if something is not working as they expect, they should plan again and modify what they are doing. When they have completed the model and have a working light, ask them to write an evaluation on the activity sheet 'Our lighthouse review' (also available as a Word® file).

Differentiation
More confident: Challenge the children to make a circuit where the light revolves, using a model kit.
Less confident: Check that the children know how to make the circuit. If necessary, simplify the circuit to just a battery and a bulb.

Review
Ask the children to place their models on their tables along with a copy of the activity sheet 'Review of the models' (also available as a Word® file). Invite them to move from table to table, trying out the lights and writing a review of each model onto the activity sheet. Remind them that what they write needs to be positive and helpful to the makers of the model. Ask questions such as:
- *What did you see that made you think that the model was made carefully?*
- *What about the electric circuit? Did that work well?*
- *How did you judge that?*

Display the activity sheet 'Sam's lighthouse'. Ask:
- *What did Sam do well?*
- *What do you think he needs to do to make his model work?*
- *Why do you think the light stopped working?*

Now try this...
Challenge the children to make another model, this time with wheels that turn, using an electric motor and a model kit to drive the wheels. Children can use activity sheet 'Our model' to plan their model and its electrical circuit.

CD-ROM follow-up material
Provide copies of the activity sheet 'Height of lighthouses'. The children make a bar chart of the data using the bar chart tool in the Kids Zone of the CD-ROM. First they must decide the scale for their chart, as there is quite a range of heights. They can decide to include the lighthouse of Alexandria or not, and to add heights of other lighthouses they can find.

Sam's lighthouse

■ Read these reviews of Sam's lighthouse.

Name	How well does the light work?	How well is the model made?	What could be done to improve the model?
Yousef	It flickered when I tried it.	Really well. I like the colours you used to paint it.	Look at your circuit. Something must be loose.
Marc	The light did not come on at all.	Loved the colours, especially the bands of red near the top.	Check your circuit. Think a wire has come undone.
Sally	The light does not work.	The model is beautiful.	Make the light work.
Ying Mai	The light is broken.	You have made a lovely shape for your lighthouse.	Mend the light.

Sentence types

Mathematics learning objectives
Framework:
- **HD:** Answer a set of related questions by collecting, selecting and organising relevant data; draw conclusions, using ICT to present features, and identify further questions to ask.
- **NC:** Ma4, 1a; Ma4, 2a–b

English learning objective (NC)
- **En3, 7b:** The features of different types of sentence, including statements, questions and commands, and how to use them (for example, imperatives in commands).

Vocabulary
Bar chart, chart, range

Resources
- Fiction and non-fiction books

CD-ROM:
- Activity sheets: 'Examples of sentences' 1–3, 'Questions in news stories' 1 and 2 (also p15), 'Notes for a story' and 'Advertisements'
- Interactive tables: 'Sentence examples' and 'Words to begin sentences'
- Word® file: 'Examples of sentences'
- Bar chart tool

Introduction
Display the interactive table 'Sentence examples'. Ask the children to read the first sentence. Point out the headers (Statement, Question, Command) and ask them to decide to which category this sentence belongs. If the children do not agree, discuss what type of sentence it is and how to tell. Add a mark to the 'Statement' column once everyone has agreed that this is correct. Repeat this with the other sentences. Ask:
- *How can you tell if a sentence contains a question?*
- *What about a command? What is a key feature?*
- *How many commands are there here?*
- *What does each command begin with?*

Display the interactive table 'Words to begin sentences'. Ask the children to give you a sentence beginning with each word. After each sentence, discuss the sentence type. In groups, ask the children to compile a list of other words to begin each type of sentence. Add their suggestions to the table. Continue to display the table. Ask the children to write their own statement, question and command sentences. Review these together.

Children's task
Ask the children to work in pairs. Provide each pair with a fiction or non-fiction book and a copy of the activity sheets 'Examples of sentences' 1–3 (also available as a Word® file). The pairs look for examples of statement, question and command sentences and add these to the sheet, with an explanation for each sentence saying why it belongs in the column they have chosen.

Differentiation
More confident: Challenge the children to find more complex sentences and to identify where these fit.
Less confident: Decide whether to work with the children, perhaps using a piece of on-screen text. Children work together to find the various types of sentence.

Review
Invite the children to give examples of each type of sentence and to explain why they have classified each sentence in their chosen way. Ask:
- *How do you know that this sentence is a statement/ question/command?*

Display the activity sheets 'Questions in news stories' 1 and 2. These contain two bar charts, each of which shows the number of questions that were asked during a different week of news programmes. Ask the children to study each chart, then ask, for example:
- *What do you notice about the scales of the two charts?*
- *Which chart do you think is easier to read? Why?*
- *What is the range for the first chart?*
- *What is the mean average of questions asked for that chart?*
- *Look carefully at the second chart. What do you notice about the numbers of questions asked?*
- *Why do you think this was?*

Now try this...
Provide children with the activity sheet 'Notes for a story'. Read the instructions. Ask the children to write the story. When they have finished, they share their story with a partner, discussing the number of sentences which were statements, questions or commands.

CD-ROM follow-up material
The top table on activity sheet 'Advertisements' shows the number of sentence types that were found in 50 advertisements. Ask the children to complete the totals for each type, then to make a bar chart to show the totals, using the bar chart tool in the Kids Zone of the CD-ROM. They can then record their own data from advertisements and from a range of TV programmes in the second table.

Questions in news stories

■ Paul and Mark counted the number of questions asked in the 6pm news programme on television. Here are the results for one week.

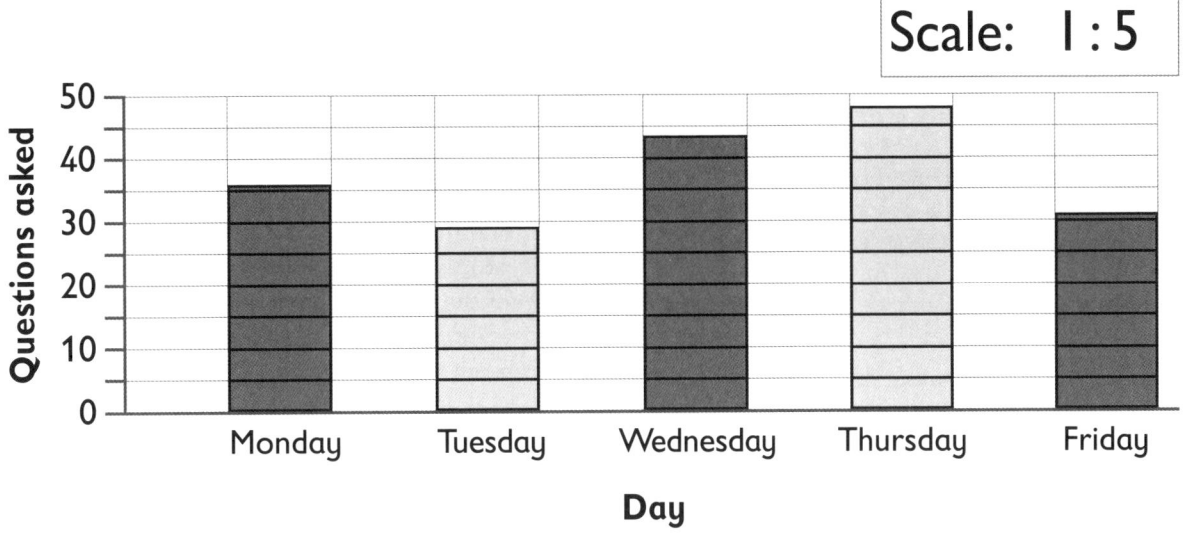

Scale: 1 : 5

■ They repeated this for the 1pm news. Here are the results for one week.

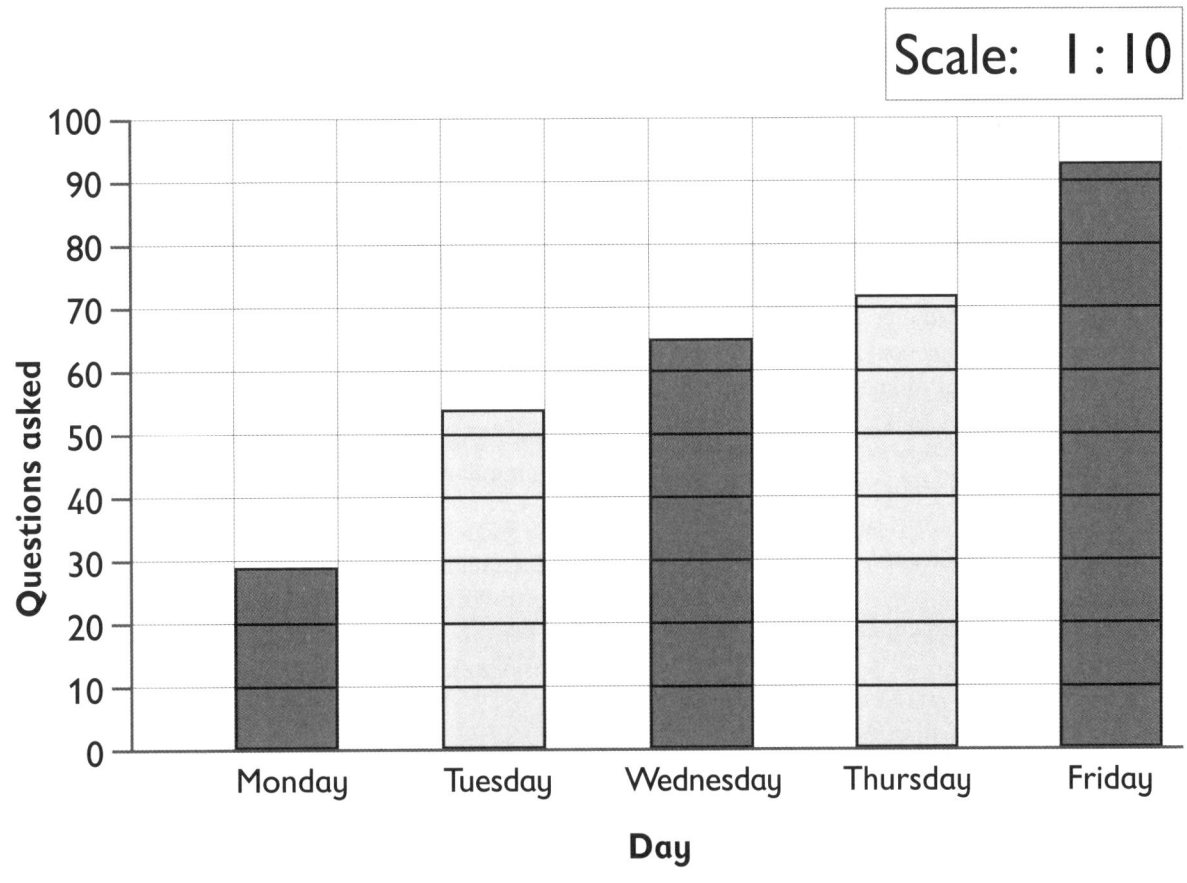

Scale: 1 : 10

15

Mumbai and London

Mathematics learning objectives
Framework:
- **HD:** Answer a set of related questions by collecting, selecting and organising relevant data; draw conclusions, using ICT to present features, and identify further questions to ask.
- **HD:** Construct frequency tables, pictograms and bar and line graphs to represent the frequencies of events and changes over time.
- **NC:** Ma4, 1a; Ma4, 2c–d

Geography learning objectives (NC)
- **6a:** A locality in the United Kingdom.
- **6b:** A locality in a country that is less economically developed.

Vocabulary
Bar line chart, maximum value, minimum value, range

Resources
- Atlases, digital camera or scanner, books about travel
CD-ROM:
- Activity sheets: 'Data' (also p17), 'Climate of Mumbai', 'Climate of London', 'Blank bar line chart' and 'Edinburgh and Cardiff'
- Images: 'Mumbai' 1–3 and 'London' 1–3

Introduction
Ask the children to use their atlases to find Mumbai. If children are unsure, explain that Mumbai is the capital of the Indian state of Maharashtra. Next, ask the children to find London in their atlases. Display the images of Mumbai and London and then the activity sheet 'Data'. Look at the first table and ask:
- *Which city has the larger population/area…?*
- *If 77.45% of the population of Mumbai can read, what percentage cannot read?*
- *What do you notice about the size of each population and the areas that the cities occupy?*

Look at the second table. Ask, for example:
- *By how much has the population of India grown from 2001 to now?*
- *By how much has the population of England grown in the same period?*

- *Which country has the more dense population?*
- *Why do you think that?*

Children's task
Provide the children with the activity sheets 'Climate of Mumbai', 'Climate of London', and 'Blank bar line chart'. Explain to the children that it is possible to draw two sets of temperature data onto the same chart by starting the line at the minimum temperature for the month and finishing it at the maximum temperature. Ask the children to make charts of the temperatures and the rainfall for both cities. There are questions to answer for both cities about maximum and minimum values, and the ranges of the data. For London temperatures, children will need to realise that another region of the chart will be needed in order to show the negative numbers. If necessary, teach this so that the children can make suitable charts.

Differentiation
More confident: Challenge the children to find the same sort of climate data for another city, such as Durban. They can compare all three sets of data.
Less confident: Decide whether to ask the children to concentrate on one set of data, such as that for Mumbai.

Review
Either upload completed bar line charts to the class computer, or photograph or scan the charts. Display some Mumbai rainfall charts. Ask children to read the title, then the scale, and ask questions such as:
- *Is the title suitable? Why do you think that?*
- *What scale was used? How do you know that?*
- *So, what is the minimum rainfall?*
- *Which month was that?*

Repeat this for the other charts. Discuss how to read the temperature charts where the bar shows the maximum and the minimum. Discuss how children decided to set up their y-axis so that they could show the negative numbers. Discuss how to read the minimum temperature and the maximum temperature for each month.

Now try this...
Ask the children to choose another place, such as their home town, or a town that they have visited on holiday. Ask them to find as much data about the town as they can, using books and the internet to help them.

CD-ROM follow-up material
Provide children with the activity sheet 'Edinburgh and Cardiff'. Ask them to look carefully at the data showing the average amount of sunshine and rainfall each month for each city. Suggest they answer the questions in pairs and explain their answers to question 5 to each other.

Data

Data about Mumbai and London

	Mumbai	London
Population	13,830,884	7,556,900
Literacy	77.45%	99%
Area of city	437.1km^2	1,572.1km^2
Compulsory education	10 years	11 years

Data about India and England

	India	England
Population now (estimate)	1,189,998,000	52,000,000
Population in 2001 census	1,028,610,328	49,138,831
Total area	3,287,240km^2	130,395km^2

Greece then and now

Mathematics learning objectives
Framework:
- **HD:** Answer a set of related questions by collecting, selecting and organising relevant data; draw conclusions, using ICT to present features, and identify further questions to ask.
- **HD:** Construct frequency tables, pictograms and bar and line graphs to represent the frequencies of events and changes over time.
- **HD:** Find and interpret the mode of a set of data.
- **NC:** Ma4, 1a; Ma4, 2c

History learning objective (NC)
- **12:** A study of the way of life, beliefs and achievements of the people living in Ancient Greece and the influence of their civilisation on the world today.

Vocabulary
Bar line chart, chart, maximum value, minimum value, range

Resources
- School software for creating bar line charts, internet access and a digital camera or scanner
- **CD-ROM:** 💿
- Activity sheets: 'Using the products of the olive tree', 'Olive trees across the world' (also p19), 'Olive tree yield', 'Blank bar line chart', 'Wine', 'Pottery', 'Imports and exports' and 'Holiday visitors'
- Bar chart tool; Pie chart tool

Introduction
Discuss how in Ancient Greece farmers grew olives. Display the activity sheet 'Using the products of the olive tree'. Ask the children to compare Ancient Greece with today and to note that the uses are very similar. Discuss how there are still olive trees in Greece which are thought to be about 2000 years old.

Display the activity sheet 'Olive trees across the world'. Look at this carefully. Discuss what the table shows. Ask:
- *Which country uses the largest area to grow olives?*
- *Which country produces the largest tonnage of olives?*
- *Which country grows the most olives for each hectare under cultivation?*

Children's task
Provide copies of the activity sheets 'Olive tree yield' and 'Blank bar line chart' (or access to the bar chart tool in the Kids Zone of the CD-ROM). Ask the children to make a bar line chart using this data. Remind them that this data has been corrected to two decimal places so they will need to think carefully about the scale that they choose. The children then re-write the table, ordering the yields from smallest to largest. They find the minimum and maximum values of the yields and the range. When the children have finished, suggest they discuss their work with a partner and ask each other questions.

Differentiation
More confident: The children can research other olive-producing countries to add to the chart.
Less confident: If necessary, help the children to further correct the figures to one decimal place. This may help them with identifying what scale to use.

Review
Scan and upload (or photograph) one of the completed bar line charts to the class computer. Display the bar line chart and ask:
- *What scale was used? How do you know this?*
- *Do you agree with the scale that was chosen?*
- *Why do you think this?*
- *Which country produces the least amount of olives for each hectare under cultivation?*
- *Which countries produce more than Syria but less than Greece?*

Discuss how the children found the minimum and maximum values of the yield and the range.

Show the activity sheet 'Wine'. Discuss the medical uses of wine. Ask the children whether doctors today would prescribe wine for these purposes. Now display the activity sheet 'Pottery'. Ask the children to look carefully at the image and to describe what they can see.

Now try this...
The children can find out about the Ancient Greeks and maritime trading and use the internet to research what the Greeks exported and imported. They can record their research findings on 'Imports and exports'.

CD-ROM follow-up material
Provide children with the activity sheet 'Holiday visitors', which contains data about the number of tourists to visit various countries. With a partner, children can make a bar line chart and a pie chart from the information using the relevant tools in the Kids Zone of the CD-ROM and compare the two to decide which is easier to interpret.

Olive trees across the world

■ Look carefully at this data.

Country	Production in tons	Cultivated areas in hectares	Yield for each hectare in tons
Spain	6,204,700	2,500,000	24.82
Italy	3,600,500	1,159,000	31.07
Greece	2,444,230	765,000	31.40
Turkey	1,290,654	727,503	17.74
Syria	885,942	635,691	13.94
Morocco	770,000	550,000	14.00
Tunisia	750,000	2,300,000	3.26
Egypt	500,000	110,000	45.45
Algeria	475,182	288,442	16.47
Portugal	362,600	380,700	9.52
Argentina	160,000	52,000	30.77

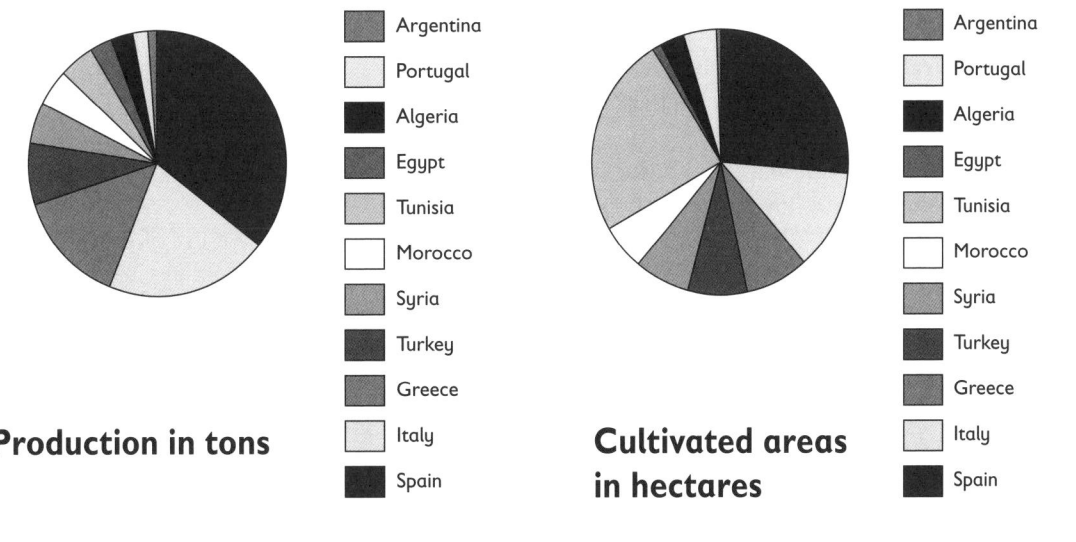

Production in tons

Cultivated areas in hectares

Legend (both charts): Argentina, Portugal, Algeria, Egypt, Tunisia, Morocco, Syria, Turkey, Greece, Italy, Spain

Spreadsheets

Resources
- Excel® or similar spreadsheet software, catalogues and internet access

CD-ROM:
- Activity sheets: 'Traffic passing our school' (also p21), 'Holiday costs', 'Data collection chart' and 'Fun day out'

Introduction
All instructions for using spreadsheets are for Excel®; if your school uses simpler spreadsheet software, the instructions will be similar. The lesson will involve using and making spreadsheets, it assumes that children have some knowledge of how they work. Display the spreadsheet on 'Traffic passing our school'. Ask:
- *What is in cell A3/B3…?*
- *What goes in column A/column B?*

Ask the children to calculate mentally the sum of column B. Display the chart on 'Traffic passing our school'. Ask:
- *What is the scale of this chart? How can you tell that?*
- *Do you think this is an appropriate scale? Why?*

Open Excel® or your spreadsheet software and enter the data from page 21. Demonstrate how to total the column of figures by typing into cell B7, the box below the final number: =B2+B3+B4+B5+B6 and press return. The total should appear in cell B7. Now demonstrate how to make a chart from this data. In Excel®, go to

Charts then click Column. This will produce the bar chart which can be dragged with the mouse to where it is required. Similarly, selecting Bar will produce a bar chart. Next, demonstrate the multiplication function. Click in cell C2 and type: =B2*2 and press return. Explain that this has multiplied 45 by 2.

Children's task
Provide activity sheet 'Holiday costs' to pairs of children, so that they can discuss what they are entering and why. Children use the data to make a simple spreadsheet. They enter data for each person, names in one column and costs in the next. Then they total the costs using the add formula. Finally, they find the total cost of going for twice as long using the multiplication formula.

Differentiation
More confident: Challenge the children to show on their spreadsheet the cost for going on holiday for two, three and four weeks.

Less confident: Decide whether to work as a group. Children can observe how to enter the data before trying it themselves. Likewise, they can observe how to total then multiply, then do this for themselves.

Review
Upload and display one of the completed spreadsheets. Ask the children to explain how they undertook the task and have a child demonstrate how to total a column of numbers. Ask another child to demonstrate how to multiply using the formula. Ask:
- *How do you think you would total two numbers?*
- *How do you think you would find the difference between two numbers?*
- *How do you think you would divide a number by (for example) 2, using a formula?*

In each case ask a child to demonstrate. To total two numbers: =A1+A2 and return; to find the difference: =A1–A2 and return; to divide a number by 2: =A1/2 and return. Invite other children to demonstrate how to total, multiply, subtract and divide further numbers.

Now try this...
Ask the children to make a list of five DVDs and five music downloads they would like to own. They find and record price information on the activity sheet 'Data collection chart' and then enter it onto a spreadsheet.

CD-ROM follow-up material
Activity sheet 'Fun day out' gives data for three fun days out. The children make a spreadsheet to show the costs for six children and two adults and the total cost for each day out. They can also cost different combinations of people.

Scholastic Data Handling   Year 5

Traffic passing our school

Spreadsheet

■ This spreadsheet shows the amount of traffic that passed a school in a measured amount of time.

	A	B
	Traffic	**Frequency**
1		
2	Cars	45
3	Buses	13
4	Motorcycles	4
5	Bicycles	6
6	Lorries and vans	3

Bar chart

■ This bar chart has been created from the spreadsheet above.

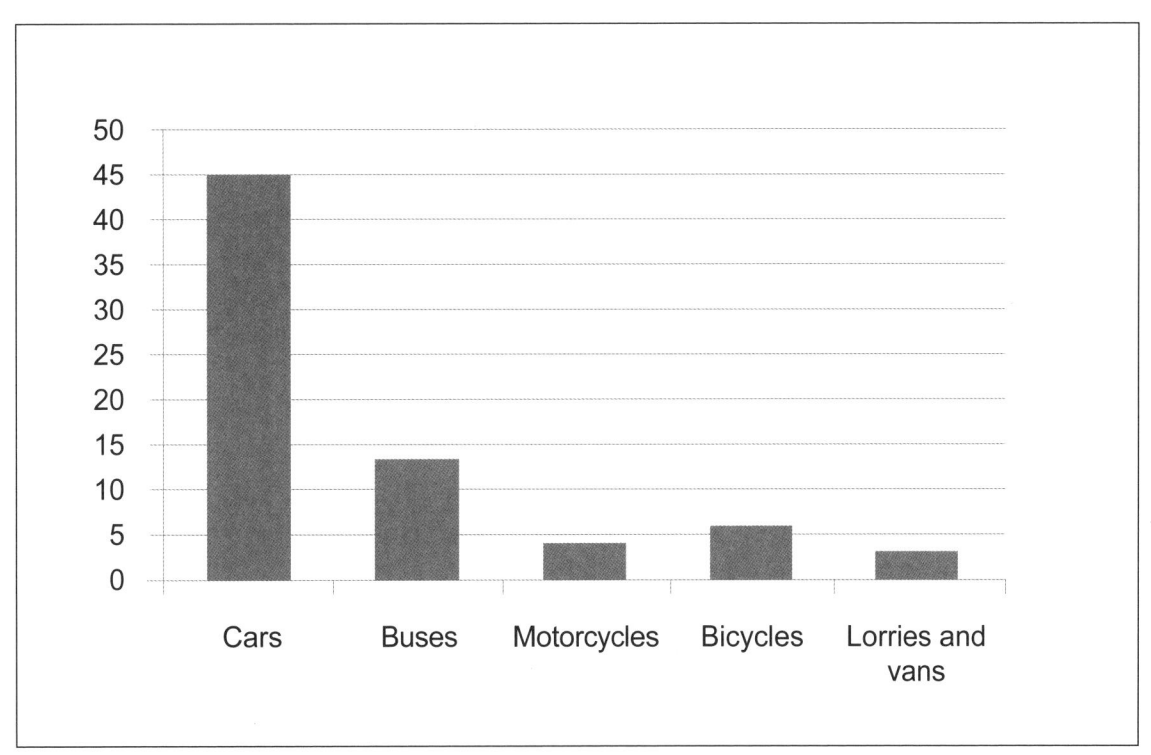

Music review

Mathematics learning objectives
Framework:
- **HD:** Answer a set of related questions by collecting, selecting and organising relevant data; draw conclusions, using ICT to present features, and identify further questions to ask
- **HD:** Find and interpret the mode of a set of data.
- **NC:** Ma4, 1a; Ma4, 2b

Music learning objective (NC)
- **5e:** A range of live and recorded music from different times and cultures (for example, from the British Isles, from classical, folk and popular genres, by well-known composers and performers).

Vocabulary
Bar chart, chart, maximum value, minimum value, mode, range

Resources
- Recordings of various pieces of music, word-processing or desktop-publishing software, spreadsheet or database software, books about music and internet access

CD-ROM:
- Activity sheets: 'Music review' (enlarged to A3), 'Favourite composers' (also p23), 'Pop music review' (enlarged to A3) and 'Pop music from the 1960s'
- Bar chart tool

Introduction
Provide copies of the activity sheet 'Music review'. Explain that you will be playing some music for the children to listen to and then review. Write the composer and name of the piece on the board. Play the music. Ask the children to sit quietly and think about how the music made them feel. Ask them to write their thoughts onto the sheet. Ask:
- *What did/didn't you like about this music and why?*
Repeat this for the other pieces of music.

Children's task
Ask the children to work in pairs at a computer. Using their notes on 'Music review', they type a review for each piece of music, beginning a new page for each review. Each review begins with the name of the composer and the piece of music being reviewed, followed by the review. Encourage the children to add design features. Create a class display in a common area, if possible with a recording of the music so that others can listen and read the reviews.

Differentiation
More confident: Challenge the children to write more detailed reviews, including feelings that the music evoked.
Less confident: Decide whether to ask an adult to work with this group. The adult can help them to clarify what they liked or did not like, and why.

Review
Write a list of the pieces that the children listened to on the board. Ask them to be ready to vote for their favourite. Remind them that they may have only one vote. Write the votes onto the board. Display the bar chart tool and explain that you are going to make a bar chart of their votes together. Invite one child to type in the music names along the x-axis; another child to decide on the scale, and a third to input the data. Discuss the chart produced and ask:
- *Do you think that the best scale was chosen? Why?*
Ask the children to write down the voting numbers, in order, starting with the least number of votes. Then ask them to find the minimum and maximum values, the range, and the mode of the data.

Display the activity sheet 'Favourite composers'. Ask the children to look at the bar chart; explain that it was made in Excel®. Ask:
- *Do you think the scale that the computer software chose was a sensible one? Why do you think that?*
Now ask the children to find the minimum and maximum values of the data, the range and the mode.

Look together at the pie chart. Ask:
- *Who was the most/least popular composer?*
- *How many votes do you think each composer had? Can you tell that from this pie chart?*

Now try this...
The children can repeat this activity, this time for pop music, using the activity sheet 'Pop music review'. They can make a class database of their responses.

CD-ROM follow-up material
Provide copies of the activity sheet 'Pop music from the 1960s'. Ask the children to enter the data into a spreadsheet and to make a bar chart of their data. They can then research 1970s music, complete the sheet and make a bar chart of that data.

Favourite composers

■ Class 5B's votes made this bar chart.

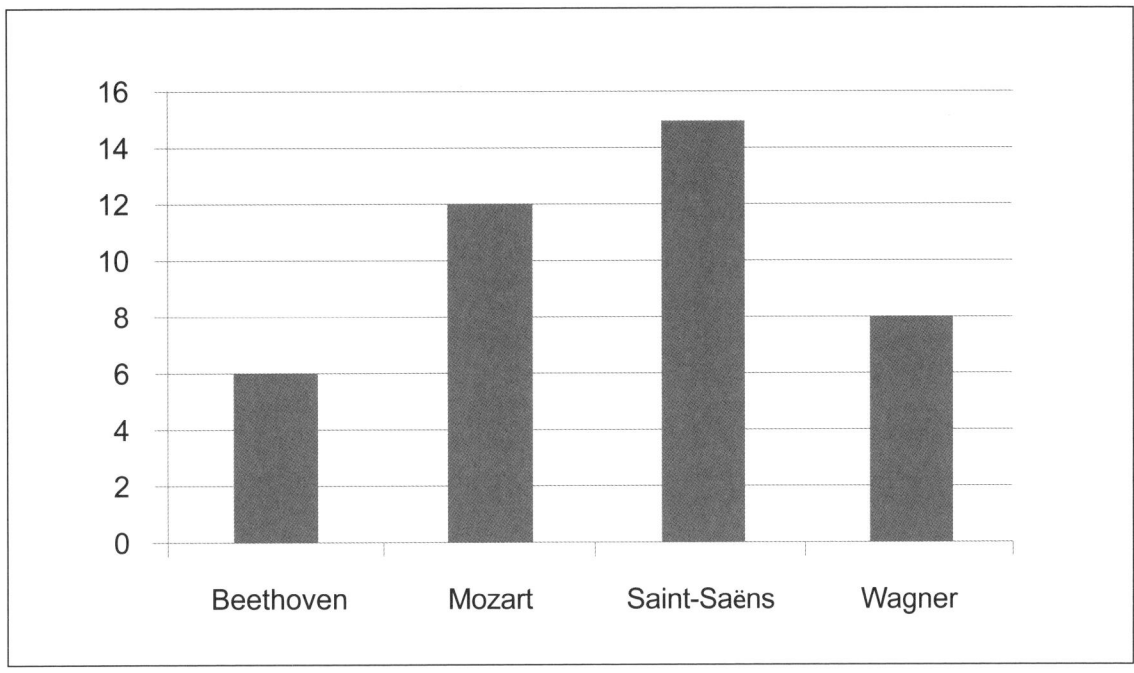

■ Class 5C's votes made this pie chart.

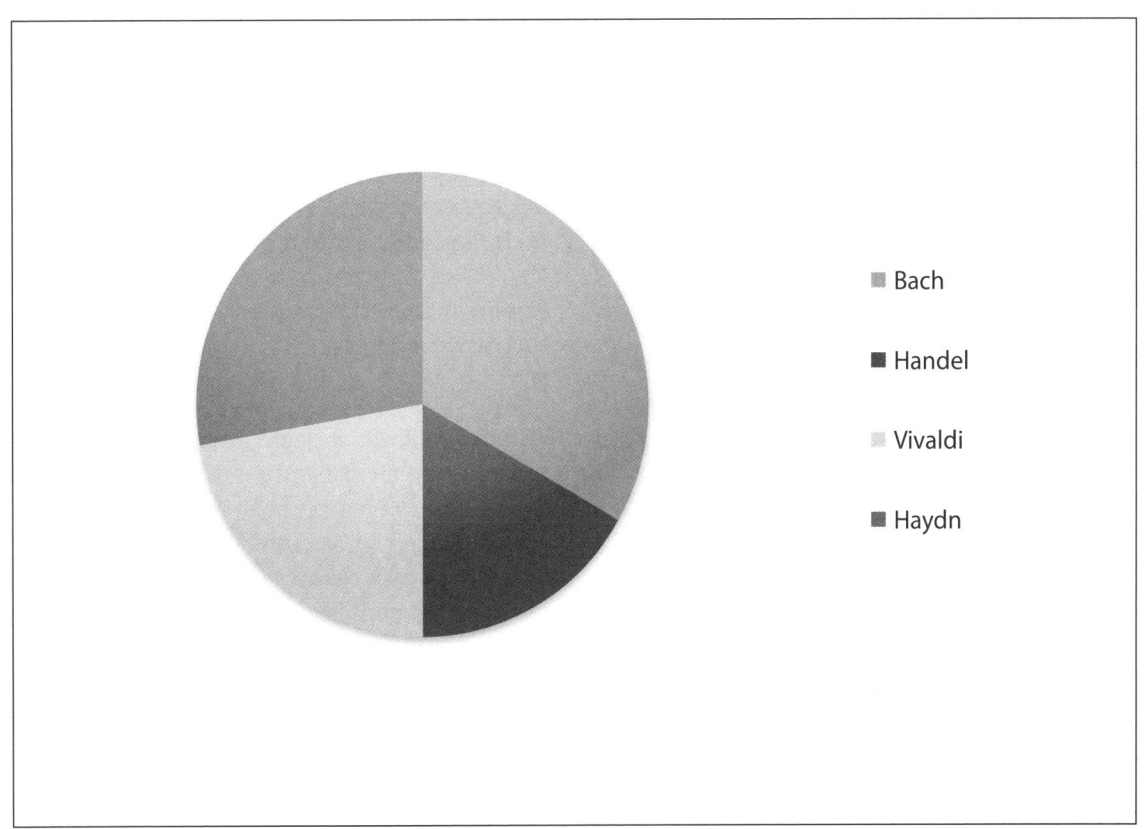

Bach
Handel
Vivaldi
Haydn

Names in the 1930s

Mathematics learning objectives
Framework:
- **HD:** Find and interpret the mode of a set of data.
- **NC:** Ma4, 1a; Ma4, 2d

History learning objective (NC)
- **2b:** About the social, cultural, religious and ethnic diversity of the societies studied, in Britain and the wider world.

Vocabulary
Bar line chart, mode, range

Resources
- Digital camera and internet access

CD-ROM:
- Activity sheets: 'Top ten names in the 1930s' (also p25), 'Names in the 2010s', 'Names bar line chart' and 'Baby names from 2010'
- Word® file: 'Names in the 2010s'
- Bar chart tool

Introduction
Display the first chart from the activity sheet 'Top ten names in the 1930s'. Ask the children to look carefully at the names; then ask, for example:
- *Which of these names do we still use for children today?*
- *Is anybody in your family named Donald or Betty?*
- *Which do you think would have been the most popular boy's/girl's name in the 1930s?*
- *Why do you think that?*

Now display the second chart. Ask the children to look at it carefully and explain that the names are now in popularity order. Ask questions such as:
- *Why do you think Mary was such a popular name?*
- *How many more girls were called Mary than Betty?*
- *How many more boys were called John than William?*
- *In total how many children were named Mary and Robert?*
- *What does the chart tell you about the number of babies born in the 1930s?*

Children's task
Ask the children to survey the class to collect names. They will need one or more copies of the activity sheet

'Names in the 2010s' (also available as a Word® file). Ask them to work in groups of four and to complete the chart for that group. Then they move to a different group and repeat this. Do this several times until all the children have all of the names. Decide whether the children are collecting first names only or whether they should add middle names too. Be sure that they are clear which names they are recording and counting. When the children have all of the names, ask them to find the mode and range of their data. They make a bar line chart of their data to show the popularity of the names, using the activity sheet 'Names bar line chart'. Children could also survey another class or the whole year to obtain more data.

Differentiation
More confident: Challenge the children to collect more data, such as collecting names from another class. They compare the mode and range for the two classes' names.
Less confident: Decide whether to limit the work to collecting names from their group, tallying these, and finding the mode and range.

Review
Photograph and upload to the class computer a completed frequency table and a bar line chart. If children have completed a frequency table for another class, upload this too. Display the completed frequency table for your class and ask, for example:
- *Which is the most popular boy's/girl's name?*
- *How many girls/boys have that name?*
- *What is the mode of the data? How did you work that out?*
- *What is the range of the data? How did you calculate that?*

Display the bar line chart and ask, for example:
- *Is the chart easy to read and interpret?*
- *Why do you think that?*

Repeat this for the frequency table for another class or the year, if available.

Now try this...
Ask the children to search the internet to find the 100 most popular first names in the 1920s, 1940s, 1960s, and so on. Children can compare charts of different decades to spot which names remain popular and for how long. They could also research and compare popular names in different countries.

CD-ROM follow-up material
The activity sheet 'Baby names from 2010' contains the top ten names for boys and girls for one month in 2010. Children can make bar line charts of the data, using the bar chart tool in the Kids Zone of the CD-ROM, then answer some questions. They can then find the most popular babies' names for the previous year using the internet.

Scholastic Data Handling **Year 5**

Top ten names in the 1930s

In alphabetical order

Boys	Girls
Charles	Barbara
Donald	Betty
George	Dorothy
James	Helen
John	Joan
Joseph	Margaret
Richard	Mary
Robert	Nancy
Thomas	Patricia
William	Shirley

The number of each name chosen

Rank	Boys		Girls	
	Name	Number	Name	Number
1	Robert	31,079	Mary	29,397
2	James	29,048	Betty	15,234
3	John	25,818	Barbara	15,156
4	William	22,215	Shirley	11,719
5	Richard	17,488	Patricia	11,382
6	Charles	16,020	Dorothy	10,958
7	Donald	14,944	Joan	8925
8	George	10,307	Margaret	8100
9	Thomas	9767	Nancy	7208
10	Joseph	9651	Helen	7165

25

How long did you take?

Mathematics learning objectives
Framework:
- **HD:** Construct frequency tables, pictograms and bar and line graphs to represent the frequencies of events and changes over time.
- **HD:** Find and interpret the mode of a set of data.
- **NC:** Ma4, 1a; Ma4, 2a–d

Physical education learning objective (NC)
- **2a:** Plan, use and adapt strategies, tactics and compositional ideas for individual, pair, small-group and small-team activities.

Vocabulary
Bar line chart, database, mode, range

Resources
- Stopwatches, PE equipment such as balls, hoops and skipping ropes, local newspapers and/or internet access

CD-ROM:
- Activity sheets: 'Olympic medals table 1912' (also p27), 'Timings table', 'Blank bar line chart', 'Olympic medals table 1968', 'Olympic medals – 1912 and 1968' and '2008 Olympic data' (1 and 2)
- Images: 'Runners' 1–4
- Bar chart tool; Pie chart tool; Table tool

Introduction
Show the images from the CD-ROM and discuss the range of sports that are held at the Olympic Games. Explain that, in 1912, results were recorded with basic stopwatches, and that from 1968 onwards the results were recorded using electronic timing, which is much more accurate. Display the activity sheet 'Olympic medals table 1912'. This table shows the top ten medal winners in the 1912 Olympics. Ask the children to write down the total number of medals won, in order, from least to most. When they have finished ask:
- *Which country won the most medals in total?*
- *What is the range of the total number of medals won?*
- *How did you work that out?*
- *What is the mode of the total number of medals won?*

Children's task
Explain to the children that you would like them to work in groups of four. They plan three PE activities, such as running 50m, throwing and catching a ball 20 times. They choose one of the tasks, and each try it three times. They record their times on the activity sheet 'Timings table'. If there is time, they try the other two tasks in the same way. Back in the classroom the children find the range and mode of their scores for the tasks they have completed. They then work together to compare each other's scores. Taking each person's best score they find the mode and range for their group, and make a bar line chart, using the activity sheet 'Blank bar line chart' or the bar chart tool in the Kids Zone of the CD-ROM. When making bar line charts remind the children to include the scale that they have chosen.

Differentiation
More confident: Challenge the children to use a digital stopwatch that gives time to two decimal places. Ask them to take readings as accurately as they can, and to find the mode and the range of these.
Less confident: Decide whether to work with the children to find the range and the mode of the data.

Review
Review with the children the data that they have collected. Ask them to explain, for example:
- *How did you find the mode/range of this data?*
- *Does anyone have a larger range than this?*
Display both activity sheets 'Olympic medals table 1912' and 'Olympic medals table 1968'. Ask the children to look carefully at the gold medal winners; then ask questions for each year such as:
- *What is the mode for the gold/silver/bronze medals?*
- *How did you find the mode?*
- *Why do you think that the USA came top of the medals table in both years?*
- *How many medals were won in total?*

Now try this...
Children can find out more about race results from local sports clubs which involve timings. They devise their own table to collect the data, using the table tool in the Kids Zone of the CD-ROM. Ask them to find the range and mode of the data and make bar line charts, choosing appropriate scales and titles.

CD-ROM follow-up material
Provide pairs with copies of the activity sheets '2008 Olympic data' 1 and 2. Ask the pairs to read and discuss the data, and answer the questions. They can enter the data into a spreadsheet and make bar line and pie charts using the relevant tools in the Kids Zone of the CD-ROM and compare them for ease of use.

Olympic medals table 1912

■ This table shows the top ten medal winners in the 1912 Olympics.

Rank	Nation	Gold	Silver	Bronze	Total
1	United States	25	19	19	63
2	Sweden	24	24	17	65
3	Great Britain	10	15	16	41
4	Finland	9	8	9	26
5	France	7	4	3	14
6	Germany	5	13	7	25
7	South Africa	4	2	0	6
8	Norway	4	1	4	9
9	Canada	3	2	3	8
10	Hungary	3	2	3	8

Water

Mathematics learning objectives
Framework:
- **HD:** Answer a set of related questions by collecting, selecting and organising relevant data; draw conclusions, using ICT to present features, and identify further questions to ask.
- **HD:** Construct frequency tables, pictograms and bar and line graphs to represent the frequencies of events and changes over time.
- **NC:** Ma4, 1a; Ma4, 2b–c

Personal, social and health education learning objective (NC)
- **2j:** That resources can be allocated in different ways and that these economic choices affect individuals, communities and the sustainability of the environment.

. . . .

Vocabulary
Bar line chart, data, range

Resources
- School water meter with adult supervision and internet access
CD-ROM:
- Activity sheets: 'Using water at home' (also p29), 'School use of water', 'Blank bar line chart', 'How much water?' and 'Bottled water'
- Images: 'Water' 1–3
- Video: 'Water meter'
- Bar chart tool

Introduction
Display and discuss the water images and the video. Discuss the difference between having a water meter (paying for usage) and the old water system (paying a fixed price, regardless of usage). Ask the children if they shower or bathe. Record the results on the board. Display the activity sheet 'Using water at home'. Ask:
- *How many more litres does a bath use than a shower?*
- *Does this matter? Why?*
- *What else can you tell me from the table?*

Speak to the school caretaker for permission for children to take readings from the school water meter. Deputise children to go in pairs, with the caretaker, and take a reading daily until they have ten days of readings. They record their data on the activity sheet 'School use of water'. The children make a bar line chart, using the activity sheet 'Blank bar line chart' or the bar chart tool in the Kids Zone of the CD-ROM, to show the water usage for the ten days.

Children's task
This is a homework task, to be completed over a week; the children complete the activity sheet 'How much water?' As this includes toilet-flushing it may be advisable to inform families of this homework and ask for their cooperation. At the end of the week, discuss with the children the range of values they have recorded in order to set the scale on a class bar line chart. Ask the children to enter their data onto the chart.

Differentiation
More confident: Challenge the children to look at other uses of water at home and to encourage the family to measure this out, where possible.
Less confident: Decide whether to limit the range of the task. The children could collect data on the number of baths or showers and make a group chart of their results.

Review
Display the chart showing water usage in school. Ask:
- *Do we use about the same amount of water each day?*
- *How much water do we use in a school week?*
- *How did you work that out?*

Now ask for feedback about water usage at home:
- *Were your family surprised by how much water was used?*
- *How many of you have a water meter at home?*
- *Did you check how much more you used than what you recorded?*
- *What other uses of water are there at home?*

Display the class bar line chart of home water usage. Some homes will have used far more than others. Ask:
- *What is the smallest/largest quantity of water used?*
- *So what is the range of this data?*

Now try this...
Ask children in groups to discuss how we waste water. For example, does a dishwasher use less water than washing up by hand after each meal; how much water is flushed away each day for a household?

CD-ROM follow-up material
The children collect data on how much bottled water is drunk in school in a week and record it using the activity sheet 'Bottled water'. They use the data to make a chart showing daily consumption, calculate the cost by checking current prices from supermarkets and compare this with current prices for water by checking online.

Using water at home

■ Look at the table below. It shows how much water is used during some everyday activities.

■ Now, answer the questions.

Action/appliance	Amount of water used each time (litres)
Old washing machine	181.6
Modern washing machine	90.8
Having a shower	90.8
Having a bath	136.2
Flushing the toilet	8.0
Washing up each day	63.0
Using the dishwasher	25.0
Washing the car with a bucket and sponge	32.0
Washing the car with a hose	400.0

■ 5 litres of water out of the tap costs about 1p.

1. Work out how much it costs to wash the car with a bucket and sponge.

_____

_____

_____

_____

2. Work out how much it costs to wash the car with a hose.

_____

_____

_____

_____

Feelings

Mathematics learning objectives
Framework:
- **HD:** Answer a set of related questions by collecting, selecting and organising relevant data; draw conclusions, using ICT to present features, and identify further questions to ask.
- **NC:** Ma4, 1a; Ma4, 2b

Personal, social and health education learning objectives (NC)
- **3f:** That pressure to behave in an unacceptable or risky way can come from a variety of sources, including people they know, and how to ask for help and use basic techniques for resisting pressure to do wrong.
- **4a:** That their actions affect themselves and others, to care about other people's feelings and to try to see things from their points of view.

Vocabulary
Chart, data

Resources
- Access to the internet
- **CD-ROM:** 💿
- Activity sheets: 'Which behaviour?' (also p31), 'What would you do?' 1 and 2, 'Anti-bullying' and 'American schools in 2007'
- Word® file: 'Anti-bullying'

Introduction
Explain to the children that in this activity they will explore their feelings about their and other people's behaviour. Display the activity sheet 'Which behaviour?' Ask the children to read the first story and each of the four scenes. Ask them to discuss the scenes in pairs, then groups of four, then eights. Ask questions such as:
- *How do you think Sam would feel if he behaved as in scene 1/2/3/4?*
- *How do you think the child being bullied would feel?*
Repeat this for the other four stories, each time asking the children to describe what they think both the bully and the child being bullied must be feeling.

Children's task
Provide copies of the activity sheets 'What would you do?' 1 and 2. Ask the children to work in pairs to read through each story and discuss the three scenes. They decide which option they would choose and why, then they discuss how the bully must be feeling and how the victim must be feeling. They write their responses on the activity sheets. Remind the children that they are not expected to always be 'Goody Two-Shoes', but rather they should explore their feelings, and how such behaviour is likely to affect other people.

Differentiation
More confident: Ask the children to write their own scenarios and give three different scenes that might follow. They discuss these with their partner.
Less confident: Decide whether to ask an adult to work with the children. Encourage the children to discuss the scenes each time and to explore the feelings of the bully and the victim in detail.

Review
Ask the pairs to combine into groups of four to discuss their responses to 'Which behaviour?' and decide who will feed back to the class. Ask questions such as:
- *How do you think the child being bullied feels?*
- *How do you think the big brother feels?*
- *Why do you think the child being bullied bullies others?*
Ask the children to discuss in their groups what they think will happen if they tell a teacher about a bullying incident they have witnessed. Ask, for example:
- *What do you think the teacher will do?*
- *What would you like the teacher to do?*
- *Why would you like this to happen?*
If children give negative responses, discuss with them the duty that teachers have with regard to bullying.

Now try this...
Ask the children to think of some anti-bullying activities. They might, for example, set up bully boxes where children can put a note if they are too frightened to speak out about what is happening. They could consider a buddy system to work with younger children. The children can record their ideas for helping to stamp out bullying at school on the activity sheet 'Anti-bullying' (also available as a Word® file).

CD-ROM follow-up material
Provide copies of the activity sheet 'American schools in 2007'. Explain that this data is about secondary school pupils. Explain also that each bar is a percentage of all the children in school of that age. In pairs or groups of four, ask the children to look at the data and answer the questions. Then, ask the children to research UK statistics on bullying in schools.

Scholastic Data Handling   Year 5

Which behaviour?

- Read the first story. Then read each of the four scenes.
- Discuss the scenes with your partner, then with a bigger group.
- Do this with the other four stories.

Story	Scene 1	Scene 2	Scene 3	Scene 4
Some popular children dare Sam to throw a biscuit at one of your friends in the class.	Sam throws it and says sorry later.	Sam throws the biscuit and laughs.	Sam refuses to do it.	Sam tells the teacher.
Sam sees one of his friends hitting another child at playtime.	Sam joins in the fight.	Sam helps his friend with the hitting.	Sam helps the victim and tells the friend to stop.	Sam watches.
A class bully threatens Jan because Jan saw her cheat in a test.	Jan walks away and worries about it all day.	Jan tells her parents or teacher.	Jan threatens the bully because she won't carry out the threat.	Jan talks to her best friend about it.
Jan goes online and sees someone she doesn't like is online too. Jan writes a threatening message. The other child complains about the message to the teacher.	Jan pretends she did not hear the teacher.	Jan tells the truth even though she may get into trouble.	Jan insists it was not her.	Jan lies and says the child is making up the story.
You see a bully from your class being punched and kicked by his big brother.	Do you laugh and think he is getting what he deserves?	Do you talk to your teacher about it?	Do you pretend you didn't see what was happening?	What else could you do?

Google Earth®

Mathematics learning objectives
Framework:
- **HD:** Answer a set of related questions by collecting, selecting and organising relevant data; draw conclusions, using ICT to present features, and identify further questions to ask.
- **NC:** Ma4, 1a; Ma4, 2b

Geography learning objectives (NC)
- **2c:** To use atlases and globes, and maps and plans at a range of scales (for example, using contents, keys, grids).
- **2d:** To use secondary sources of information, including aerial photographs (for example, stories, information texts, the internet, satellite images, photographs, videos).

. . . .

Vocabulary
Database, data

Resources
- Google Earth®, Excel® or similar school spreadsheet/database software
- **CD-ROM:**
- Activity sheets: 'Distances between towns' (also p33), 'A journey plan', 'Travel database' and 'Journeys'
- Excel® file: 'Distances between towns'
- Table tool

Introduction
Display the first database on the activity sheet 'Distances between towns' (also available as an Excel® file). Ask the children to look carefully at the database; then ask:
- *How long does it take to get from Manchester to Liverpool going through Bolton?*
- *What is the total journey time from Manchester to Bolton, then to Liverpool, then back to Manchester?*
- *What is the total distance travelled?*

Ask similar questions about the other two databases.
Reveal Google Earth® on the class computer. Demonstrate how to fly to a location, then travel to another one, and where they can find the distance travelled and time taken. The children make a journey from where they live to a city, going via somewhere else.

The children will need to know how to make a database using the school's database software. Demonstrate this, putting in the details from the Google Earth® journey, including the time and distance for each leg of the journey. Show the children how to total the distances. Discuss how times will need to be in hours and decimal fractions of an hour for the database to total them. Remind the children how to make a decimal fraction of minutes.

Children's task
Ask the children to work in pairs with a copy of the activity sheet 'A journey plan'. Ask them to plan a journey which takes them through three major towns in Britain, then back to their starting point. They use Google Earth® to find and record the distance and time taken for each leg of their journey. Encourage them to 'travel' large distances, such as from London, through Birmingham, Manchester and Preston, to Carlisle.

When they have completed their three journeys using Google Earth®, ask the children to work individually to set up a database with their journey data in it. From the database they should be able to total the distance and the time taken for each journey. Display the activity sheet 'Travel database' and ask the children to discuss the questions with a partner.

Differentiation
More confident: Challenge the children to plan longer journeys with more places to visit en route.
Less confident: Children may be more confident with making a journey with just one stop en route.

Review
Ask the children to describe some of the journeys they made and what their total distance was. Discuss how they totalled the distance using the database software. Review the time some of the journeys took and why. Discuss how they arrived at their conclusions and how Google Earth® and the databases helped them.

Now try this...
Using Google Earth®, the children 'travel' from home to a foreign capital city or a holiday destination. They use the table tool to record data and make a class chart of holiday destinations with driving times and distances.

CD-ROM follow-up material
Distribute the activity sheet 'Journeys'. Ask the children, in pairs, to follow each journey, find the totals and discuss the questions. They use Google Earth® to find out how long the direct journey back from Llandudno to Southampton would take and how far this is. The children can then compare this data with a route back using different stops from those in the 'Journeys' data.

Distances between towns

	A	B	C	D
1	**From**	**To**	**Distance in miles**	**Time**
2	Manchester	Bolton	16.7	28 minutes
3	Bolton	Liverpool	36.0	52 minutes
4	Liverpool	Manchester	35.7	52 minutes

	A	B	C	D
1	**From**	**To**	**Distance in miles**	**Time**
2	Hereford	Newport	46.6	54 minutes
3	Newport	Bristol	31.1	39 minutes
4	Bristol	Hereford	65.5	1 hour and 20 minutes

	A	B	C	D
1	**From**	**To**	**Distance in miles**	**Time**
2	Edinburgh	Glasgow	46.7	59 minutes
3	Glasgow	Falkirk	24.6	35 minutes
4	Falkirk	Stirling	13.7	23 minutes
5	Stirling	Edinburgh	36.2	55 minutes

Life in Ancient Greece

Mathematics learning objectives
Framework:
■ **HD:** Answer a set of related questions by collecting, selecting and organising relevant data; draw conclusions, using ICT to present features, and identify further questions to ask.
■ **NC:** Ma4, 1a; Ma4, 2b

History learning objective (NC)
■ **12:** A study of the way of life, beliefs and achievements of the people living in Ancient Greece and the influence of their civilisation on the world today.

• •

Vocabulary
Bar chart, chart

Resources
■ Internet access, books about life in Ancient Greece and Google Earth®

CD-ROM:
■ Activity sheets: 'Class 5's research – 1' (also p35), 'Life in Ancient Greece' (enlarged to A3), 'Class 5's research – 2', 'Slaves' lives' and 'Distances from Athens'
■ Word® files: 'Life in Ancient Greece' and 'Slaves' lives'
■ Images: 'Pottery' 1–4, 'Jars', 'Oil lamps' and 'Vase'
■ Bar chart tool

Introduction
Explain that the children will be researching life in classical Ancient Greece. Display the images and discuss how pottery often showed scenes from everyday life. Display the activity sheet 'Class 5's research – 1'. Say that Class 5 used books and the internet to research some aspects of life in Ancient Greek times. Ask:
■ *What other facts do you know about these times?*
■ *Which of the old Greek stories have you heard or read?*
■ *Are these the same pets that you keep?*
■ *Why do you think the Greeks did not keep cats as pets?*
■ *What job do you think the cats did for humans?*
Explain that charts like this can be used to gather evidence before writing in full what has been found out. Tell the children that, when using charts, they can write in note form, perhaps using bullet points to show where each new idea begins.

Children's task
Provide copies of the activity sheet 'Life in Ancient Greece', which covers aspects of life in Ancient Greece different from those you have been looking at. Provide books and access to computers for research purposes. If computers are readily available, children can complete their notes on the Word® file; then print these out.

Differentiation
More confident: Challenge the children to find out about men's and women's lives in Ancient Greece, both inside and outside the home.
Less confident: Decide whether to limit the topics that children research to, for example, children's lives and education.

Review
Choose one or two charts that are well structured, perhaps using bullet points to show where a new idea begins. Display these and ask questions such as:
■ *How do the bullet points help you with making notes?*
■ *How do the bullet points help you with reading your notes when you are ready to write up what you have found out?*
■ *Look at these notes on children's lives/education... What else did you find out?*
■ *Would you have liked to live in Ancient Greece? In Athens or Sparta?*
Display the activity sheet 'Class 5's research – 2'. Ask the children to read the notes carefully. Ask:
■ *Did you find out about any of these things when you did your research?*
■ *Look at the notes about men's lives. What do you think the men traded?*
■ *Which hobbies are similar to those of men today?*
■ *Does anything surprise you about women's lives?*
■ *What is similar about women's lives in Ancient Greece and now?*
■ *What would you not have liked about women's lives? Why is that?*

Now try this...
The children research the lives of the slaves: where they came from; what work they were expected to do; and how their masters and mistresses treated them. The activity sheet 'Slaves' lives' can be used to record their findings (a Word® version is also available).

CD-ROM follow-up material
The activity sheet 'Distances from Athens' shows how far Athens is from some major Ancient Greek sites. Provide access to Google Earth®. Ask the children to plot routes from Athens to each site, to find the travel time, and then to use the bar chart tool to make a chart to show the distances. They can answer the questions with a partner.

Class 5's research

■ This chart shows Class 5's notes on their research on Ancient Greece.

Research by Class 5

Religion	• Worshipped many different gods, such as Zeus, Apollo, Athena and Poseidon. • They believed gods looked like humans but had superhuman strength and never aged.
Grave art	• A coin to pay Charon, the ferryman to Hades, was placed in the hand of the dead person so that they could cross the river. • There were animal sacrifices at the funeral. • They gave a special speech called an epitaphio. This is where we get our word 'epitaph' from.
Pets	• They kept birds, dogs, tortoises and mice. • They did not keep cats.
Dancing	• They believed that dancing was good for their health. • Men and women did not usually dance together. • Men danced with men and women danced with women in some dances.
Stories	• They had many fabulous stories, myths and fables that we still enjoy today.

Friction

Mathematics learning objectives
Framework:
- **HD:** Answer a set of related questions by collecting, selecting and organising relevant data; draw conclusions, using ICT to present features, and identify further questions to ask.
- **NC:** Ma4, 1a; Ma4, 2b

Science learning objective (NC)
- **Sc4, 2c:** About friction, including air resistance, as a force that slows moving objects and may prevent objects from starting to move.

Vocabulary
Bar chart, table

Resources
- Toy car, ramp, measuring tape, stopwatch and materials for the car to run along from the ramp such as carpet, vinyl floor covering, paper and so on, and access to the internet

CD-ROM:
- Activity sheets: 'Effects of friction', 'John's results', 'Stopping distances' 1 and 2 (also p37), 'Friction' and 'Bobsleighing data'
- Interactive table: 'Our car results'
- Word® file: 'Friction'

Introduction
Explain to the children that in this lesson they will be considering friction. Begin by showing them the toy car, the ramp and the materials for the car to run along. Place a piece of carpet at the end of the ramp. Ask:
- *How far do you think the car will run from the ramp? Why?*
- *How much friction do you think there will be?*

Invite a child to let the car run down the ramp, without pushing. Ask another child to measure how far the car runs, and a third child to time how long the car runs along the carpet. A fourth child can enter the results into the interactive table 'Our car results'. Discuss the units to be used when entering the results, for example, decimal fractions of a metre, decimal fractions of a minute. Repeat this for the other surface materials. Ask:
- *Which surface offered the greatest friction effect?*

- *How do you know that?*
- *Which one offered the least friction effect?*
- *How much difference in distance travelled/time taken do you think the different levels of friction made?*

Children's task
Ask the children to work in pairs to complete the table on the activity sheet 'Effects of friction'. Ask them to add other things that they can think of that are affected by friction. For example, a spacecraft gets hot entering the Earth's atmosphere due to air friction; butter helps a knife to 'slide' across toast because of low friction. Ask the children to be prepared to discuss their decisions.

Differentiation
More confident: Ask the children to think of more unusual things. For example, what difference does the type of swimwear that athletes use make to their performance in swimming? What difference does the type of tyres used on cars in Formula 1 make, depending upon the weather conditions?
Less confident: Decide whether to work with this group. The children may need support in identifying some of the effects of friction.

Review
Ask the children to take turns to read out what they wrote on the activity sheet 'Effects of friction'. Discuss answers where children disagree. Review what else children added to their sheet, asking questions such as:
- *Why do you think that is so?*
- *Who agrees/disagrees? Why?*

Display the activity sheet 'John's results'. Ask the children to look at each of John's suggestions. Discuss his answers. The children will have their own thoughts and suggestions, so it may help to ask the questions above.

Display the activity sheets 'Stopping distances' 1 and 2. Ask pairs to look at the data and answer the questions. Ask them to discuss their findings with another pair and to talk about how useful the bar chart was.

Now try this...
Ask the children to look at home for items that grip, slip, slide and so on. They record these items on the activity sheet 'Friction' (also available as a Word® file). There are some ideas on the sheet to help them get started. They can compare their list with others'.

CD-ROM follow-up material
Provide the activity sheet 'Bobsleighing data'. Ask the children to look at the data and answer the questions. Then they can search on the internet for results for other sports where friction can affect the results, such as skating, skiing and so on.

Stopping distances

■ These are the results of some tests on cars and lorries to find out how long they take to stop when they brake.

Vehicle	Weight in tonnes	Braking distance in metres	
		30mph	45mph
Car	1.3	7.26	18.00
Small van	1.4	7.14	25.36
Bomb disposal vehicle	10.9	11.07	26.19
Armoured personnel carrier	6.9	16.79	28.14
Bus	36.0	20.68	31.30
Dump truck	15.0	18.90	23.11

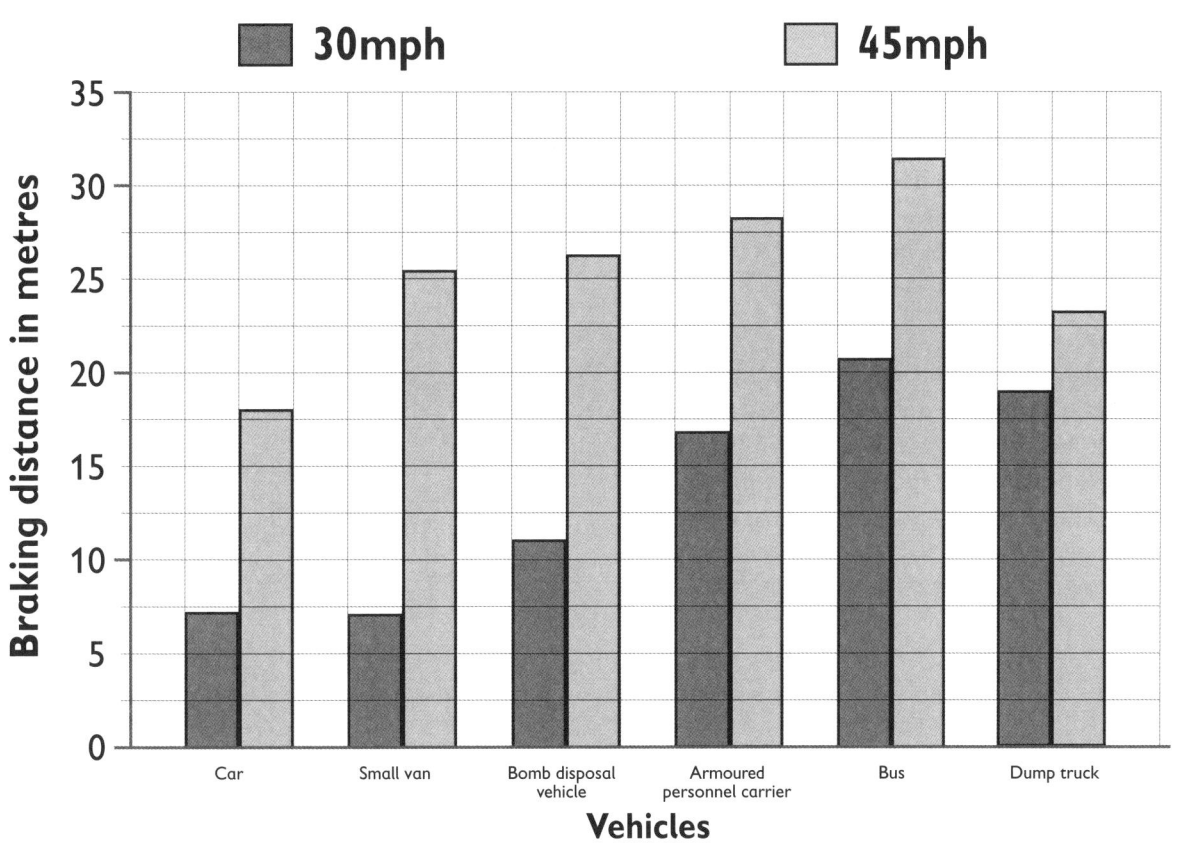

PHOTOCOPIABLE ■SCHOLASTIC
www.scholastic.co.uk

Make a bag

Mathematics learning objectives
Framework
- **HD:** Answer a set of related questions by collecting, selecting and organising relevant data; draw conclusions, using ICT to present features, and identify further questions to ask.
- **HD:** Find and interpret the mode of a set of data.
- **NC:** Ma4, 1a; Ma4, 2b–c

Design and technology learning objective (NC)
- **3b:** Carry out appropriate tests before making any improvements.

. . . .

Vocabulary
Bar line chart, maximum value, minimum value, mode, range

Resources
- Newspaper, glue sticks, sticky tape, weights, scissors, fabric, sewing equipment and access to the internet

CD-ROM: 💿
- Activity sheets: 'Make a bag', 'Test a bag', 'Group test results' (also p39) and 'Recycling energy savings'
- Images: 'Tag', 'Notebook', 'Paper bag' and 'Water bottles'
- Bar chart tool

Introduction
Explain that the children will be making bags with handles, using newspaper, glue and sticky tape. Discuss how to make strong shapes when designing and making. Ask:
- *How could you make your bag strong?*
- *What could you do to strengthen the handles?*
- *You will be testing your bags by putting weights into them. Where do you think the weak places will be?*

Children's task
Give pairs of children the activity sheet 'Make a bag', scissors, glue sticks, sticky tape and newspaper. Ask them to read the sheet and work together to design their bag. Explain that it will be tested to destruction to find out how strong it is. The children may try out some designs, to check on strength and durability. Encourage them to improve their designs and keep their 'workings out'.

Provide groups of eight with a copy of the activity sheet 'Test a bag'. As they will be loading the bags with weights, ask them to think about the safety issues. Ask:
- *What will happen to the weights when the bag breaks?*
- *In what ways could this cause damage or hurt someone?*
- *So how will you ensure everyone's safety whilst testing?*
Children may suggest raising the bag a few centimetres from the floor and placing a tray under the bag to catch weights. Check that they do this safely. They record the load in each of the four bags on the activity sheet. Children may need reminding that they should put in as much weight as they think the bag will safely hold to begin with, then add weights until it breaks.

Set up a class bar line chart using the bar chart tool on the CD-ROM. The children enter the maximum weights that their bags held before breaking.

Differentiation
More confident: Challenge the children to explore the class chart and find maximum and minimum values of final weights, and to find the range for the class.
Less confident: Decide whether to ask an adult to work with the children to think about safety and design.

Review
Display the class bar line chart and ask questions such as:
- *What is the scale? How do you know that?*
- *What is the minimum/maximum weight that a bag held just before it broke?*
- *What is the range/mode of these values?*
Invite the children to evaluate what they made. Ask:
- *How could you improve your bag?*
- *If you made it again what would you do differently?*
Display the activity sheet 'Group test results'. Ask:
- *At what weight did each bag break?*
- *What is the range/mode of the largest weights that the bags held?*
- *At what weight did James'/Emily's bag break?*

Now try this...
The children can design and make bags by sewing fabric, thinking about strength and durability. They can calculate the front panel area of their bag, compare this with others to find the range of sizes, and make a chart of their results.

CD-ROM follow-up material
Provide copies of the activity sheet 'Recycling energy savings' and access to the images from the CD-ROM. Explain that in recycling materials, energy still needs to be used. Ask the children to answer the questions, if necessary doing some internet research.

Group test results

■ These tables show the results from two groups' bag tests.

Swallows

Name	Test 1	Test 2	Test 3	Test 4	Test 5	Test 6	Test 7
James	1.0kg	1.2kg	1.40kg	1.600kg	1.8kg	1.90kg	
Sunil	0.5kg	0.6kg	0.75kg	0.800kg			
Fleur	1.5kg	2.0kg	2.20kg	2.300kg	2.4kg		
Mia	2.0kg	2.1kg	2.15kg	2.175kg	2.8kg	2.85kg	2.9kg
Fred	0.6kg	0.7kg					

Robins

Name	Test 1	Test 2	Test 3	Test 4	Test 5	Test 6	Test 7
Mo	1.2kg	1.4kg	1.6kg	1.8kg	1.9kg	2.0kg	2.1kg
Aran	0.5kg	0.7kg	0.8kg	0.9kg			
Zack	1.5kg	2.0kg	2.5kg				
Emily	1.6kg	1.8kg	2.0kg	2.2kg	2.3kg	2.4kg	
Alfie	1.6kg	1.9kg	2.2kg	2.5kg	2.8kg		

Sports heroes

Mathematics learning objectives
Framework:
- **HD:** Construct frequency tables, pictograms and bar and line graphs to represent the frequencies of events and changes over time.
- **NC:** Ma4, 1a; Ma4, 2b–c

Physical education learning objective (NC)
- **3a:** Identify what makes a performance effective.

Vocabulary
Bar line chart, line graph, table

Resources
- Calculators, stopwatches that read in seconds, sports equipment as needed and access to the internet

CD-ROM: 💿
- Activity sheets: 'The Pentathlon – 1' (also p41), 'Pentathlon practice', 'Blank line graph', 'The Pentathlon – 2' and 'Combined sports' 1 and 2
- Images: 'Modern Pentathlon' 1–3 and 'Pentathlon' 1–3
- Line graph tool; Bar chart tool

Introduction
Explain that the children will be looking at sporting heroes. Begin with the Pentathlon, meaning five competitions/events. Explain that this originated at the Ancient Greek Olympics and consisted of the long jump, javelin, and discus, followed by the *stadion* (a short foot race) and wrestling. The men who took part in this sport were considered by the Ancient Greeks to be the best athletes, and the training was often done as part of their military service, as the skills developed were considered appropriate for a soldier. The modern Pentathlon focuses on the skills required by a late 19th-century soldier, consisting of five events: shooting, swimming, fencing, show-jumping, and cross-country running. Compare the images of the original Pentathlon events with the modern ones.

Display the medal tables for the 2008 Pentathlon from the activity sheet 'The Pentathlon – 1' and ask:
- *Who won the Russian gold medal, a man or a woman?*
- *How many gold/sliver/bronze medals were won in total?*
- *Who won the medal for Britain, a man or a woman?*

Children's task
Ask the children to think of activities that could make up a class Pentathlon. List their suggestions on the board. Encourage them to decide which five suggestions would make a manageable and achievable Pentathlon to try. For example, if they include swimming it has to be in the summer term. Encourage them to include some simpler events, such as running 50m or skipping for 20 turns of a rope. Once the five activities have been agreed, ask the children to work in pairs to practise them, time each other, and log their times on the activity sheet 'Pentathlon practice'. If possible, hold a Pentathlon event, where the children try out their skills and are given their final times. The children should convert their times into decimal fractions of minutes, by dividing the seconds by 60 (they may need to use a calculator). They then use the activity sheet 'Blank line graph' or the line graph tool in the Kids Zone of the CD-ROM to make a line graph of each of the activities to show how they have improved.

Differentiation
More confident: Ask the children to use stopwatches that read the seconds as decimal fractions; for example, the reading might be 1 minute and 54.6 seconds. They convert this to a decimal fraction of a minute.
Less confident: The children may need help with converting the times to decimal fractions of a minute.

Review
Discuss the children's results and how they have improved. Some may prefer to do this individually without other children listening.

Display the results for 1968 from the activity sheet 'The Pentathlon – 2'. Ask questions such as:
- *Which was Jim Fox's best event?*
- *Who had the best score for running?*
- *Did this person win the overall competition?*
- *In which sports did Björn Ferm have the best results?*

Now try this...
Ask the children to review the results for local modern Pentathlon events. There may well be a local club for this sport. They read the tables of results and work out who won which event. They could make a bar line chart using the bar chart tool in the Kids Zone of the CD-ROM to show the total scores of the top four or five contestants.

CD-ROM follow-up material
Provide copies of the activity sheets 'Combined Sports' 1 and 2. Explain that 'OR' stands for 'Olympic Record'. Ask the children to make a bar line chart for each of the results tables to show the points that each country won. They can search the internet to find the scores for each of the individual events and make a table of the results.

The Pentathlon – 1

Men

Rank Men	Country	Gold	Silver	Bronze	Total
1	Russia	1	0	0	1
2	Lithuania	0	1	1	2

Women

Rank Women	Country	Gold	Silver	Bronze	Total
1	Germany	1	0	0	1
2	Great Britain	0	1	0	1
3	Ukraine	0	0	1	1

Combined

Rank Combined	Country	Gold	Silver	Bronze	Total
1=	Germany	1	0	0	1
1=	Russia	1	0	0	1
3	Lithuania	0	1	1	2
4	Great Britain	0	0	0	1
5	Ukraine	0	0	1	1

Price comparisons

Mathematics learning objectives
Framework:
- **HD:** Construct frequency tables, pictograms and bar and line graphs to represent the frequencies of events and changes over time.
- **NC:** Ma4 1a, 2b, c

Citizenship learning objective (NC)
- **1f:** To look after their money and realise that future wants and needs may be met through saving.

Vocabulary
Bar line chart, maximum value, minimum value, mode, range, table

Resources
- Local newspapers with second-hand car sales advertisements and calculators

CD-ROM:
- Activity sheets: 'Price comparison' (also p43), 'Finding the right price', 'Blank bar line chart' and 'Sweets sale'
- Bar chart tool; Table tool

Introduction
Explain to the children that in this lesson they will be considering value for money. Ask, for example:
- *How would you decide how much to pay for something?*
- *Where would you look for help?*
- *How many of you search for the best price for something you want to buy?*
- *Where would you look to find the best price?*

Display the first table on the activity sheet 'Price comparison'. Explain what each column shows: the year the car was first registered; the size of its engine; its mileage; the asking price. Ask, for example:
- *Which of these cars do you think would be value for money? Why?*
- *What else would you need to consider when buying a second-hand car?*

Discuss issues such as: the colour of the car; paintwork condition; how worn the interior is; how well it drives.

Children's task
Ask the children to work in pairs with a copy of the activity sheet 'Finding the right price'. They search through local papers for prices of cars to compare. Advise the children to look for similar cars to compare, choosing the same model name where possible. They enter their data in the table; then decide which car would be best value for money and why. They also find the range and the mode of the prices. The children can make a chart of the prices they have found using the activity sheet 'Blank bar line chart' or the bar chart tool in the Kids Zone of the CD-ROM.

Differentiation
More confident: Challenge the children to find at least ten cars to compare.
Less confident: Decide whether to work with the children to find prices and to enter these in the table. If children find working with larger numbers difficult, work together to find the range and the mode of the prices. Children can write the prices on pieces of paper and order them from least to most.

Review
Ask the children to report back on what sorts of cars they chose and the range of prices they considered. Ask:
- *What was the highest price you looked at?*
- *Was this the best value? Why do you think that?*
- *How did you choose your best value?*
- *Was the lowest price the best value? Why do you think that?*

Display the second table on the activity sheet 'Price comparison' and ask:
- *Which do you think would be the best value for money?*
- *How would you make the decision?*
- *Why do you think the 1.6 litre convertible is so much more expensive than the other cars?*
- *What do you need to think about when looking for value for money?*

Now try this...
Repeat this activity using house prices. Children can compare the prices of semi-detached houses with bungalows and detached houses, considering the number of bedrooms and so on. They can make a price table using the table tool in the Kids Zone of the CD-ROM, then make a bar line chart from their data. The numbers will be very large and children may need help with recognising the values.

CD-ROM follow-up material
Provide copies of the activity sheet 'Sweets sale', which provides full price data for wholesale sweets. Ask the children to use a calculator to find the prices after a 50% and a 25% reduction in price. They can make bar charts of the data and ask each other questions about the prices, such as finding the most/least expensive item; how much more one item costs than another, and so on.

Scholastic Data Handling **Year 5**

Price comparison

■ Compare these cars in terms of value for money.

Citroën Grand C4 Picasso™

Registration plate	Model	Mileage	Price in £
57	1.6 litre	30,000	7999
57	1.8 litre	22,000	7299
57	1.8 litre	21,000	7299
08	1.8 litre	7,000	7995
07	2.0 litre	35,000	7499

Renault Mégane™

Registration plate	Model	Mileage	Price in £
57	1.6 litre	11,000	4999
07	1.4 litre	27,000	4999
07	1.6 litre	33,000	4999
57	1.4 litre	12,000	5495
57	1.6 litre	16,000	4995
56	1.5 litre	10,000	5495
54	1.6 litre	56,000	3695
57	1.6 litre convertible	12,500	7999

Scoring goals

Resources
- Calculators, newspapers, access to the internet and Excel® or similar spreadsheet software

CD-ROM: 🎵
- Activity sheets: 'World netball series 2009' (also p45), 'Superleague netball', 'Superleague netball – answers', 'Goals scored' and '2011 Indoor Hockey World Cup' 1–7
- Word® file: 'Goals scored'
- Excel® files: 'Indoor Hockey World Cup' 1–7
- Images: 'Goal-scoring' 1–6
- Bar chart tool

Introduction
Display the images from the CD-ROM. Ask the children to name each sport, say what they know about how the game is played, and think of other goal-scoring sports.

Explain that the children will be looking at results from sporting activities. Display the activity sheet 'World netball series 2009' and ask:
- *How many matches did England/Australia/Jamaica… win?*
- *How many goals did each country score in total?*
- *In which match was the largest/fewest number of goals scored?*
- *How many matches did each team play?*
- *Who do you think won the competition? How did you work this out?*

The results were, in order of placing: New Zealand, Jamaica, Australia, England, Malawi then Samoa. Say:
- *England and Australia won five matches. Why do you think Australia was given third place and England fourth?*

Children's task
Provide copies of the activity sheet 'Superleague netball'. Ensure the children understand what each column represents. The children complete the table by finding the goal differences: in some cases these will be negative numbers in order to show that the team lost more goals than it won. The children rank the teams in order of success. (A version with answers is also available.)

Differentiation
More confident: Provide calculators and ask the children to work out the ratio of goals for/against. They divide the goals won by the goals lost. For example, Team Bath won 856 and lost 498 so the ratio is 856/498 or 1:1.719.

Less confident: Decide whether to work with the children to help them to determine if the goal difference should be represented as a negative or positive number.

Review
Review the completed activity sheets asking:
- *Which team scored the most/least goals?*
- *Which team won/lost the most matches?*
- *Who do you think won the superleague? How did you work that out?*
- *What is the maximum/minimum number of goals scored by any team?*
- *What is the range of the goals scored? How did you calculate that?*

If the more confident learners have calculated goal differences, ask them to explain how they did it. Display one of the tables showing the goal differences. Discuss the relationship between ranking and goal difference.

Now try this...
The children search newspapers and the internet for results from other sports. They use one or more copies of the activity sheet 'Goals scored' (also available as a Word® file) to rank the teams and record the results.

CD-ROM follow-up material
Provide groups with the copies of the activity sheets '2011 Indoor Hockey World Cup' 1–7 (also available as Excel® files). Check that the children understand what each column represents. Ask them to make a table of the number of goals each team scored across all the matches, using Excel® or similar spreadsheet software. They then order the teams by the number of goals scored and make a bar chart of the results. Ask them to compare the goals scored with the final results and to ask each other questions about the results. (Note: sheets 6 and 7 show the pool totals.)

World netball series 2009

■ This table shows the results for the World netball series 2009.

Country	Scored	Country	Scored	Winner
Samoa	16	England	36	England
Australia	31	Jamaica	26	Australia
New Zealand	27	Malawi	22	New Zealand
England	24	New Zealand	21	England
Samoa	22	Jamaica	30	Jamaica
Malawi	19	Australia	31	Australia
Jamaica	28	New Zealand	37	New Zealand
Australia	25	New Zealand	22	Australia
Malawi	33	Samoa	16	Malawi
Jamaica	24	England	27	England
Australia	37	Samoa	18	Australia
Malawi	22	England	33	England
Samoa	14	New Zealand	34	New Zealand
Malawi	25	Jamaica	30	Jamaica
England	25	Australia	19	England
England	22	Jamaica	33	Jamaica
Australia	17	New Zealand	27	New Zealand
Malawi	28	Samoa	20	Malawi
Australia	23	England	18	Australia
Jamaica	27	New Zealand	32	New Zealand

Erosion

Mathematics learning objectives
Framework:
- **HD:** Answer a set of related questions by collecting, selecting and organising relevant data; draw conclusions, using ICT to present features, and identify further questions to ask.
- **NC:** Ma4, 1a; Ma4, 2c

Geography learning objective (NC)
- **4b:** Recognise some physical and human processes (for example, river erosion, a factory closure) and explain how these can cause changes in places and environments.

Vocabulary
Chart, table, data

Resources
- Atlases with a good map of England, books about Britain's coastline, internet access and calculators

CD-ROM:
- Activity sheets: 'Erosion at Sizewell', 'Erosion – 1', 'Coastal erosion' (also p47), 'Erosion – 2', 'Tasmania's coastline'
- Word® files: 'Erosion' 1 and 2
- Images: 'Erosion' 1–8
- Bar chart tool

Introduction
Discuss the process of erosion along Britain's coast. Display the images. Ask the children to look at each one carefully and identify the erosion that has occurred.

Provide copies of the activity sheet 'Erosion at Sizewell'. Ask the children to read the story, then find Leiston and Sizewell in their atlases. Ask:
- *How long did it take for the erosion to take place?*
- *Do you think it will have finished now? Why?*

Explain that erosion like this has been occurring for many years. An article in The Mercury, 1880, describes a landslip at North Bay in Scarborough. The article noted that a great deal of land had gone in the previous 50 years, and that the land should be protected. In 1993, Scarborough's Holbeck Hall Hotel started to slide down the hill, seen by many on television.

The children may find the tales of Dunwich, in Suffolk, fascinating. Once a prosperous sea port, it is now mostly underwater. After huge storms in the late 13th century the town was swept into the sea over 200–300 years. The story is that at certain tides, the church bells can still be heard from beneath the waves!

Children's task
Provide copies of the activity sheet or Word® file 'Erosion – 1'. Ask the children to research the extent of erosion along the east and north-east coasts of England. Using atlases, they find towns along the coast and use books and the internet to discover which ones are affected, and how badly, by erosion. Ask the children to find out what towns have done to try to protect their coastline and the homes of the people who live there.

Differentiation
More confident: The children can find more tales about seaside towns which have suffered from erosion.
Less confident: Decide whether to limit the children to researching Felixstowe and Holderness.

Review
Invite the children to describe what they have found out about Felixstowe and Holderness. Ask:
- *What effect has the erosion had upon businesses/where people live/how they live their lives?*

Repeat this for other towns the children researched.

Display the activity sheet 'Coastal erosion'. Ask the children to read about Happisburgh and Southwold. Ask:
- *Why do you think Norfolk has stopped maintaining the erosion defences?*
- *Do you think it is expensive to defend the coast?*

Display the table at the bottom of the sheet. Ask:
- *How much erosion has there been in total from 1869 to 1966 in Highcliffe?*
- *What might have happened at Hurst Castle Spit in 1968 to make such a difference in how much land is lost from then on?*

Now try this...
Children consider other towns along the coast. They find out about the risks of erosion and record their results on the activity sheet or Word® file 'Erosion – 2'.

CD-ROM follow-up material
Provide the activity sheet 'Tasmania's coastline'. Ask the children to complete the lengths of coastline in kilometres. They may find a calculator useful for this. Then they can make a bar line chart of the lengths of coastline, in km, for each of the risks. Children may search for further data about other places at risk of erosion or flooding and make charts of their data.

Coastal erosion

How the land erodes

Town	Suffered from erosion?	What damage has erosion caused?	What has been done to minimise damage caused by erosion?
Happisburgh	Yes. The part of the village near the coast.	Houses that used to be 6m from the sea are now on the edge of the cliff and will fall into the sea.	In 1959 defences were built to stop the tide from eating away at the coast. These defences are no longer being managed and this is government policy.
Southwold	Yes, but mainly in the beach and cliff areas of the town.	Where the sea has worn away the beaches and cliffs, people have found all sorts of treasures including fossils, amber, petrified wood and the remains of salt pans.	A concrete sea wall was built about 60 years ago and this has protected the town from the sea. Rock groynes and millions of tons of sand have been added to the north beach. Worn-out beach groynes are being replaced all along the beach to give further protection from the effects of longshore drift.

■ The table below shows how much of the land or cliffs have been eroded by the sea in different locations of an area in the south-west of England.

Years	Location	How much land lost by erosion?
1869–1966	Highcliffe	0.23m
1869–1966	Lobs Hole	0.52m
1869–1966	Barton Court	0.86m
1960s	Barton cliffs	0.6–0.9m
1867–1968	Hurst Castle Spit	1.5m
1968–1982	Hurst Castle Spit	3.5m

Further ideas

Here are some further ideas for handling data across the curriculum.

Handling data	Curriculum area	Topic
Collecting information in a data chart; making notes	Art and design	Collect ideas such as images, make sketches and identify materials to use.
Collecting information in a data chart; collecting statistics and making bar line charts	Citizenship	Find out about life in another country; collect and use statistics on the weather, the temperature, the jobs that adults and older children do; make graphs or charts of their data.
Collecting information in a data chart	Design and technology	Search the internet to find ideas for a design and make project; record in a chart the materials needed, the purpose of the design, and sketch how the completed project should look.
Collecting information in a data chart	English	Use a range of newspaper reports about a particular topic: note the style of the writing, how many lines of type the topic has, which page it is in the newspaper…
Collecting information in a data chart; making bar line charts of key information	Geography	Identify the key features of two different places, analyse the evidence and draw conclusions, for example about the effect of size of population on local shops.
Storing information collected in a data chart; making bar line charts	History	Use the online census database for, eg 1901 to find out about who lived in the local area, how many people shared a house, their jobs, the number of children in a particular street…
Using the graphing feature of spreadsheets	ICT	Use a spreadsheet to calculate the cost of various items; use formulae to find the sale price of goods; make graphs of results.
Using data collection charts to record information	Music	Research the musical output of a composer or performer.
Using charts to record information	Physical education	Plan an outdoor activity challenge, such as moving through the school grounds or local park.
Using charts to record information; making bar line charts; finding mode and range of data	Science	Collect information about what is consumed by the children at lunchtime for a week; collect numerical data, eg number of bags of crisps, apples eaten; create graphs or charts, find mode and range of data.
Using charts to collect data	Personal, social and health education	Research a topical subject; use the data collected to take part in an informed debate.